INTRODUCTION

The past four months feel more like a dream than a life. I have a hard time remembering how my life felt before then. If this book is intelligible, it can only be because God's hand was on it. I have been filled, moved, changed, remade, and given what I now see as life as it was always meant to be. All this happened in months, although it feels more like years. When I think about it, my whole life has been leading up to this point. I wonder sometimes, is there anywhere else it could have led?

This book is my best attempt at describing the miraculous transformation that God is doing in me. When I started writing, I didn't understand what I was writing. The scriptures included are those that I clung to like a lifeline during the refining process. I wrote 27 Four Leaf Clovers using the help of AI. It tells the story of my life leading up to this point. Evidence, I wrote with help from the Holy Spirit. It details the battle in my mind, and how scripture, and God saw me through.

1: YAHWEH

I Am

Praise the Lord, my soul; all my inmost being praise His holy name.
Praise the Lord, my soul, and forget not all His benefits-
Who forgives all your sins and heals all your diseases,
Who redeems your life from the pit and crowns
you with love and compassion,
Who satisfies your desires with good things so that
your youth is renewed like the eagle's.
Psalm 103:2-5 NIV

What if the words in the Bible are what they claim to be? They are alive, powerful, able to divide joints and marrow, soul and spirit, capable of discerning the thoughts and intents of the heart, a weapon, a light, a history, a prophecy, the guide to understanding the past, the key to navigating the present, and the only hope for the future. What if the key to understanding is to read with belief? Believing the words are alive, speaking directly to me, and holding on to the passages that light up in my eyes, heart, and spirit. When I recognize the words for what they are, I can fully digest them, and in digesting them they begin to feed my soul. When my soul is fed by the Spirit of God, it is then able to move, see, hear, and speak in a new way. It awakens my spirit. This in turn creates a hunger that demands more.

Psalm 103:2-5 was the first verse I wrote down to memorize recently. I don't remember why or when it jumped out at me, but I wrote it down and began reciting it out loud many times a day. That one verse covers a lot of fears and doubts. When the thoughts in my head try to convince me that my past sins are still there, I remember he forgives ALL my sins. When I worry that my body is aging and I see sickness around me, I am reminded that he heals ALL my diseases. When I look around and it seems I am in a pit I can never climb out of, my spirit reminds me He rescues me from the pit and then crowns me with love and compassion. When I worry about what I will eat, how I will live, will I always feel lonely, I am reminded that He satisfies my desires with good things so that my youth is renewed like the eagles. Because I am aware of the power in the word, I am confident that it is not only true, but that it has been placed inside of me and now has authority over my life. Once I begin to acknowledge God for who He is and what He has done, my inmost being and my soul can't help but praise His holy name.

The magnitude of what I've heard and felt and realized recently, is far beyond anything my mind is capable of dreaming up. I suppose it has to be that way or I would try and rationalize away what is going on inside me. I tend to be afraid of the extraordinary in me, even though it is what I am truly seeking. I had succumb to the lie that I don't deserve the extraordinary and that to expect it is foolish.

God is truth, there is no truth apart from Him. The knowledge found in Him is undeniably more than a person could create. When I hear what God has to say, it just rings true. Like something I have always known but never realized. There is no disputing it. It just is, as it always has been, and always will be.

When I began to recognize his voice consistently in me, a new sense of self worth was awoken and my focus shifted to the internal. With the realization that the voice speaking to me is God, came the ability to digest what He speaks. How could I not be completely in awe of the voice of God speaking directly to me? This changed everything. Now every thought that passes through my mind becomes the most important part of my day. When I listen for God like this, He speaks. This is His desire, that

I listen. It is my greatest desire to hear Him speak. This is the one relationship I was created for, the realization of my greatest purpose. This is where I find the joy, peace, love, and hope I have been longing for my whole life. This is my healing, this is my perfect home, my life made whole, complete and perfect. It blots out all of the sin and disease, and covers it with what God intended.

While I wait to be taken into eternal glory, the Holy Spirit brings God's kingdom down to me. I am walking through a world full of darkness but I carry inside of me the kingdom of God. It is a light shining from within me. He is teaching me to see, hear, and walk not with my physical eyes, but with my spirit. When I walk in the knowledge that God is with me, and that He loves me in more ways than I can possibly imagine, I am emboldened. With this boldness, I am capable of finally living the life He created me to live. I no longer settle for what I have been conditioned to accept by the world.

One day as I was driving around, I began to see all the people around me doing their jobs. The trash man, tractors on the side of the highway, and cars each carrying a person driving in their lanes. It reminded me of a bunch of ants, each with their job whatever it may be inside the anthill. I have become accustomed to the fact that I am not the sole inhabitant of my mind, so the thought continued. I asked God, "How can you want to spend every second with me, an ant?" God quickly responded in the way He often does, with a question. "What if you had an ant that followed you everywhere, it hung on every word you said, it only wanted to be near you at all times, and loved you?".

As I began to think about this tiny ant looking up at me in adoration, it took no time at all before I realized how much I would treasure the ant. I would want to do whatever I could for it. Not only that, but this one ant's ability to love me would give a new value to all the ants. I would see the potential in each ant because of its likeness to my precious little adoring ant.

When God speaks, it feels like this. He doesn't have to try and explain by repeatedly saying "You are precious and loved",

4

although He does that too. When He explains something it is in a way that is irrefutable, often using my own experiences and emotions as a guide. God's love is obviously vastly beyond that of what I could possibly feel for an ant, or for anything at all. Even with my human heart I am able to grasp at a different kind of love when I ponder that ant. The love God shows me every second of every day is far beyond anything I am capable of comprehending.

I have been given a choice, the choice between life and death, the choice between unspeakable beauty or unspeakable tragedy. I have a personal Jesus, one Who has already experienced everything I will ever experience, and already paid the price for every mistake I will ever make. The price He paid was greater than I can fathom. The love He showed me before I was even born is something I can not comprehend. He took the ultimate leap and sacrificed everything for me, and then gave me the choice. I can see His sacrifice for exactly what it is, the most beautiful expression of love, one I could've never imagined. In recognizing this, my entire life, past, present, and future is changed in an instant and I am fulfilled and whole. Or I can hide from the truth of His sacrifice, running in fear and disbelief. Afraid to face the truth of who I am without Him, I can refuse to see what He has done for me. If I am brave enough to really look at my life, I have no choice but to recognize my need for a savior. When I cower in fear of my own condition I continue to inwardly rot. This turns His sacrifice into the ultimate personal tragedy. A gift so great and so costly, one that will satisfy every part of my heart and soul, turned away because of pride and fear. If someone gives their life for me, should I demand to be killed anyway out of pride, or should I accept the gift of life and then live it gratefully? Not only am I gifted life, but I am gifted a life free of sin, one filled with deep joy and peace. Should I still choose sin, pain, confusion, and fear, when I have been given joy, peace, healing, and purpose?

After 44 years of living as a christian, having grown up with the knowledge of Jesus and believing it to be true, I finally realized the power in it all. That it wasn't just a gift for eternity, and the hope isn't only for later. It is the purpose of my life now. I don't have to struggle to find my place, because He found me and carried me to it. I can tell you that nothing in my life, and I have lived a very rich and full life, has compared to the realization of my purpose and the intimate knowledge of God that comes with it. I pray that if you are reading these words they help you to find that same purpose, and if you have already found it, I hope they strengthen your faith and help you to continue walking in the spirit.

2:EL ROI

God Who Sees Me, God of Seeing

But blessed is the one who trusts in the Lord, whose confidence is in Him. They will be like a tree planted by the water that sends out its roots by the stream. It does not fear when the heat comes; its leaves are always green. It has no worries in a year of drought and never fails to bear fruit. Jeremiah 17:7-8 NIV

I am a mother of three daughters. They are now 18, 15, and 11. The lessons I have learned as a mother are innumerable. My first born, Sophia, blazing the trail, and the other two following up to make sure I don't miss anything. One of the most challenging lessons so far has been watching Sophia start to pull away and become independent. It came out in eye rolling, sarcasm, defiance and wild mood swings first. Then eventually the rollercoaster of emotions slowed down, but now I have a young adult. I soon came to realize that I had to start letting go, hoping she wouldn't go too far. I am fully aware of what is waiting for her out in the world, and also fully aware that there is no way any 18 year old is ready to navigate it alone. If I don't let go of her, she might pull further away from me in resentment, or never build the confidence needed to fully mature and thrive. I began to let go, bit by bit. I wait for her to come to me for advice, and cherish every time she does.

I suppose that is what God did for me too. Every person and every experience must be unique, but God's love is always the same. He is a good father and His character does not change. I grew up knowing God, knowing His character and that He loved me. I went 44 years not truly believing He wanted to be an active part in my life. Somehow growing up with that knowledge, I never saw the possibility that God's love and relationship with me could grow and change.

I had always come running to God in hard times, and He was always right there to meet me. Then as soon as the hard part was over, I would drift and go back to navigating life alone. I don't know why it never occurred to me that God wants to help me build my life, not just rescue me every time I fail. I had heard the words my whole life, but never truly believed them. I would only see through the eyes of faith when it was absolutely necessary to survive. It is real belief that changes everything. Real belief, the kind that made me think deeply, it opened my eyes to see and my ears to hear.

I found myself realizing that my life was half over, my kids were more than half grown and I would soon be alone with no real purpose in the world. That was the moment I let go, and that is the exact moment God was there to pick it all up. He met me where I was, and showed me how to truly follow Him. The tiny mustard seed of faith I sat on the altar, when I let go of the future I had imagined and asked for Him to take over, was all it took to start an avalanche of change. He stepped in without hesitation and led me step by step into a new life.

The second verse I wrote down immediately after the first, committing it to memory at the same time. I now have both framed on my wall, crumpled and stained, as a reminder of how all these changes began to take place. Blessed is the one who trusts in the Lord. This seems obvious, but something happened when I read the words with a desperate longing to believe. I needed to be in His blessing, and I needed to be able to trust Him. So as I began reading the words I also began to pray, "Lord help me to trust in You completely, let all my confidence be in You. I want to be like that tree planted by the stream."

Letting God's word shape my prayers gave me a confidence in prayer that I had never had before. His word clearly states that it is His will for my trust and confidence to be in Him. How could I go wrong in asking for help finding it? God delights in those who seek Him and His will, so I had every confidence that this prayer would be answered.

Sincere prayer requires bravery and trust. I know God is good and anything He does is ultimately for my good, but I also know that many times the path to answered prayer can be very difficult. Asking Him to help me trust Him, meant I would need added reasons to trust Him. This is where the knowledge of God's unending mercy and goodness are necessary. If I know everything He does is for my good, I can ask anything of Him with confidence. I know that even if it is difficult, it will always be worth it. Mercifully, He will never leave me to handle these things alone. He is always right there, ready to reassure me and help me through it all.

One night I prayed "God, I am tired of wandering through life lost. I feel like I have wasted so much time. I know you can do anything. You can make my life mean something, and you can use all my mistakes and pain for something good. Take my life. I'm giving it all to you. Just tell me what to do and I will do it. I want to make it to heaven victorious and with cheers, knowing You fully. I want to be a champion for You. I don't want to waste anymore time. I know I need work and it will be hard and it will hurt. I'm ready. Please just do it. Rip it off like a bandaid. Make me something great for You."

I heard God say "You don't know what you are asking."

I said "I know, but I know who I am asking."

I felt God smiling at me. He said "Perfect."

Today my life looks so different from the day I prayed that prayer, and it was only a few months ago. He was able to change me moment by moment because I acknowledged Him in every single moment. When I sought Him, He made Himself known to me. Knowing that He is with me in every single moment and in every single thing I do, He is able to give me wisdom in every aspect of my life.

Music is a powerful thing, it is a gift. It has the power to move me, and speak to me in a way that words alone cannot. It also has a way of sticking in my mind, not just the words and the melody but the feeling I experience with it. I have always been drawn to music, it motivates me and helps to take my mind off of everything else. I can hear a song I haven't heard in 20 years and still remember the words, and the way I felt when I listened to it all those years before. Becoming aware of what my heart and soul are glorifying as I listen has completely changed the way I listen, and the music I listen to.

Listening to countless songs that speak of the unbelievable, too good to be true experience of knowing God is priceless. They sing the testimony of so many people that are able to put into words and song, the thoughts and feelings I'm experiencing alone with God. It tells me that even though I can't see it with my physical eyes or hear it with my physical ears it is most definitely real, not just to me but to anyone who is willing to seek it. The evidence is irrefutable. Singing along to these songs my heart cries out to God in praise and prayer.

One day as I was talking to Jesus, I was talking about this vision I had of my future husband and my youngest daughter driving in the car singing along to Taylor Swift together. It is a part of the restoration I have been asking for in my life and in the life of my girls. For me to have a helper and a friend I can trust, and for my girls to have a strong and kind father figure in their lives. Anyway, it was just an image that popped in my head, and my youngest would be classified a swiftie, hence the song choice. Then I began to wonder about Taylor Swift's music, she is obviously not a fan of God. Before I could ask if it was ok to listen to it. It was like Jesus was singing "You belong with me" to me.

I had not heard this song in a very long time and had never really thought about the words. Jesus singing them to me, at this moment, could not have been more perfect. Here I was daydreaming about my future husband and He pops in with this song. I don't think I'm legally allowed to quote lyrics here but if you don't know the song look them up. It was perfect.

He in that moment not only reminded me that it is Him I need first, but He was also showing me that I could lighten up a bit. What I feed my ears and eyes is of the utmost importance, and there is a lot of music out there that I should not listen to at all. The most important thing though, is where my mind and heart are while I listen. Since that moment, I pay attention to where my mind is going when I listen to songs. Love songs make me smile in a new way because I can imagine Jesus Himself singing them to me, or me to Him. More than anything, being aware of where my focus is when I am listening or singing, lets me know if I am where I want to be. I can say with all sincerity there is nowhere I would rather be than in the presence of Jesus and with my eyes focused solely on Him. That is where I find real peace and real joy. The type of music doesn't matter all that much if it doesn't take my eyes off of Him.

Knowing God is with me when I read His word, I ask Him to help me understand. He listens when I speak and He speaks to me. He is with me as I sing to Him in praise and prayer. I am never alone. My God is the God Who sees me. Not only does He see me but He delights in me, keeps me, and cares for me in ways I may never fully understand. Knowing He sees and hears me and that He is goodness and love, my trust and confidence in Him grow immeasurably.

While I can not physically see God staring back at me, I often feel His gaze. It feels like pure emotion. I can feel Him smile at me, I can feel the look of a proud Father, I can feel His compassion when I am hurting, mostly I feel His love. If He is where all things come from, what we feel must pale in comparison to what He is. Our love, laughter, compassion, all of it must be like a foggy reflection of what He is.

Once, as I was rambling off questions to God, it made me think of the way my kids talk to me. While I love them dearly, sometimes I feel like clawing my own ears off rather than answering another question or listening to another silly story. So I asked Him, halfway laughing at the time, "Is it possible that you love me enough to actually enjoy listening to my silly questions this much? I've got to be driving you crazy." I did not hear anything back, but instantly felt this feeling of love that would be impossible for me to describe. The best way I can think to describe it is the love you feel for your children but it was whole and unhindered by any irritations or personal limitations. I instantly burst into tears. My God not only sees me, but He loves me so perfectly and He wants me to know it. He doesn't want me stumbling along through life clinging to a belief that is always slipping out of my grasp. He wants to teach me to see Him, to hear Him, and to feel Him. When I walk in the spirit, I do all three. This is the meaning of faith, walking in the spirit. He doesn't expect me to know how to do it, He shows me step by step. He wants me to seek so that I may find, ask so that I may receive, and knock so that He can open.

None of this is easy, in fact without Jesus it would be entirely impossible. Jesus gives me grace at every turn, and leads me to victory all while cheering me on in love. He makes it a mission I would be a fool to refuse, and gives me an assurance of victory long before I ever begin.

3:YAHWEH-M'KADDESH
The Lord Who Sanctifies

Now all glory to God, who is able, through His mighty power at work within us, to accomplish infinitely more than we might ask or think.
Ephesians 3:20 NLT

God can do anything, you know-far more than you could ever imagine or guess or request in your wildest dreams! He does it not by pushing us around but by working within us, His Spirit deeply and gently within us.
Ephesians 3:20 MSG

One night as I was laying in bed, I had started to drift to sleep when a strange thought drifted in my mind. It was posed like the beginning of a question. There are three of my neighbors that want a pool, and I want a pool too. We can not afford to put in a nice pool on our own. At first I thought, wow I must be tired because my mind is really drifting. Then remembering that God is with me in my thoughts, I decided to follow the strange train of thought and see where it took me. All the neighbors will pay a part of the cost of the pool and will share it. The pool can only go in one yard though. Then the question came. Would you want the pool in your yard?

If the pool goes in my yard, then my yard is now open to all of the neighbors whenever they want to use the pool. I imagine if I am willing to make such a large purchase and commitment like building a pool with these neighbors, then I must like them, so I wouldn't mind having them swimming in my backyard. The thought of the pool right outside my back door and ready to swim in whenever is very appealing. My answer is yes, I would want the pool in my yard.

Then the thought continues, won't all the neighbors want the pool in their yard? No, because if the pool is in their yard, this means they are responsible for the upkeep. It's a lot of time and energy keeping it looking nice and ready to use. Also, some of the neighbors already have lots of things in their backyards. They don't want to have to tear up what they have already built in order to put in the swimming pool.

In order to understand the context of the next part, let me explain just a little about where I was at this point in my walk with God. God had been deconstructing my entire life. Piece by piece I had been giving up every part of my day and any thought of what my future may look like had been handed over to him. This process I think is probably impossible to fully understand, even when you are in the middle of it, so it is very difficult to explain to someone who has never been through it. When I say that I am being led by God through every moment of the day, that is exactly what I mean. I have let go of everything that I was doing, all routines gone. God literally had and has me in a place of darkness. I ask him for every step. My finances were not great before, I asked him to step in, but I was working. He eventually had me let go of the job I had. I am in a place where I trust him for every penny. I had a rigorous workout routine that I enjoyed and I felt good about my body. That is gone now too. I was careful about what I ate and fasted at certain times. All of those routines are gone. Things like constant airpods, alcohol, coffee every morning and lots of it, those all went first. He has given things back, like the airpods, alcohol and coffee. When they come back it is different though. They are no longer something I have to have. They are just another step in the day when I do have them, not a ritual or routine or something I feel I need. Those things that seem like the obvious vices were easier to give up.

Giving up the job when money was tight was scary. It required a level of trust that was not automatic but had to be built before I could take that step. It was hard but not the hardest. Giving up my idea of what my future could look like, husband, farm, bliss. That one will take a lot more explaining. It was more than hurt, laying that part down, it was a kind of death. Then giving up the control I felt I had with exercise and diet was not easy, but it wasn't too bad after the whole dying thing. It was the one area that I felt like I had under control in my life. It's harder to let go when I feel like I have it going well. The money, the dream life, it was barely holding together already, otherwise I don't know if I would've been able to let it go. Maybe that's why it was at this point in my life that it all came together when everything was in a sort of shambles already.

Back to the pool thing. So I am pondering why I would be the only one who would want the pool in my backyard. One neighbor doesn't want everyone using their backyard. Another neighbor doesn't want to have to take care of the upkeep of the pool. The last neighbor has a gazebo, rose bushes, and little water features they would have to give up to make space for a pool. They love the yard they have too much to give it up. There is also going to be a lot of construction going on in my yard while it is all completed. I will have to put up with a big mess and lots of noise. I know it will be worth it though because I love to swim.

Now the scenario changed just a bit. Think of the neighbors as my brothers and sisters. My father sees that we all want a pool and that I have agreed to have it in my yard because no one else wanted it in theirs. He says he is going to pay for the pool. In fact what he is giving me is more like a full resort, and it is a lot more than I had originally planned on. It is going to be incredible, far more than I and my brothers and sisters could have ever paid for. He only asks that I treat it like it is his. Take excellent care of it and let anyone who wants to swim use it freely. Not only that, but if they come to swim, offer them food and drinks, and help take care of anyone who doesn't know how to swim well. Be an excellent host to everyone. He will keep the fridge stocked, and make sure I have everything I need. All I have to do is share what he has given me with everyone I can.

At this point the scenario turns into more of a conversation. God reminds me that when I called to Him, I was already in a very deep hole in my yard. A lot of the work had been started before I ever knew what was going on. I was ready to hand over my life to Him fully. What He is giving me in return for the muddy hole of a life I offered up, is going to be something spectacular, beyond my wildest dreams. It will require upkeep. This gift comes with responsibilities and lots of them.

I feel this overwhelming sense of gratitude. It was all far too perfect for me to create in my mind, I couldn't rationalize away what God had just spoken to me. There is no way I deserve anything so wonderful. That is the wonder of Jesus. I definitely do not deserve it, but He offers it anyway. Yes, there will be work, but the work will be rewarding, fulfilling, and good. Not only that, but I will have rewards for my work here, waiting in heaven. Also, this kind of work requires a closeness with Jesus and that is what life is all about. It really is a win, win, win scenario.

I look around my life right now with my physical eyes and see an absolute mess that I have no idea how to put back together. What my spirit sees is a construction project that is in full swing. It sees the vision that God has spoken over my life. He is not a contractor I have to keep watch over, making sure He is doing the job He promised. I can rest with Him on the job. He promises to perfect everything that concerns me. There will be no detail left out. So while it may be noisy and muddy and look very different from what it used to look like or what it will look like when it's done, I know it is all going to be better than I can imagine because of Who is in charge.

4:YAHWEH-ROHI

The Lord Our Shepherd

Do not fear, for I am with you;
Do not anxiously look about you, for I am your God.
I will strengthen you, surely I will help you, surely I
will uphold you with my righteous hand.'
Isaiah 41:10 NASB

I pulled you in from all over the world, called you in from every
dark corner of the earth, Telling you, "You're my servant, serving
on my side. I've picked you. I haven't dropped you."
Don't panic. I'm with you.
There's no need to fear for I'm your God.
I'll give you strength. I'll help you.
I'll hold you steady, keep a firm grip on you.
Isaiah 41:9-10 MSG

Fear is torment. If you have ever experienced a panic attack you know there is nothing quite as terrible. Pain is uncomfortable, but it is the fear that accompanies pain that holds the real torment. I am no stranger to loss and pain. They are something to be moved through. They have upended my life and completely changed the way I see the world on more than a few occasions. In loss and pain there is a choice. I can choose to see it as a wrong done, something stolen, which means it will probably be just one of many more wrongs that have been or will be done to me. Or I can choose to see the pain and loss as part of something bigger, acknowledging the very limited viewpoint that is the human condition.

With the first option I am a victim, entirely powerless and

at the mercy of either chaos or cruelty. This mentality breeds fear. If I look closely enough at the root of misery it is fear. God reminds us continually to not fear, the spirit of fear is not from him. I know that God's word is true, and therefore I should not be in fear. If I am experiencing fear, I need to look at why and remove it from my life. God is always happy to weed out fear in my life if I let Him. I just have to be brave enough to look with Him, trusting He is bigger than the fear.

When pain and loss have shown up in my life, that is the one time I have always gone running to God. Like a little kid running to a parent to fix something that feels like the end of the world. He has always been waiting there with open arms. He never greets me with I told you so, or some rebuke. Instead, it is always love and reassurance and mercy. There is a place in God's arms that I have felt only amid unimaginable pain and loss. God's grace, mercy, and love pour out in such a way that even the deepest wounds can become a blessing if I let them. This is how God takes the tragedy of sin and makes it work for my good.

The Lord is my Shepherd. This means He is with me caring for me in every way. He keeps me safe, feeds me, gives me a place to rest, and if I wander off He always comes to lead me back. I can not wander so far that He doesn't see me. It isn't possible. If He lets me wander, He knows right where I am and will never let me stray too far. He wants me strong, rested, fed and living with Him.

Every morning I wake up and my thoughts go to Him. I can feel Him there coaxing me awake. Some mornings He nudges me awake gently, letting me know there are things to tackle right away, some mornings He lets me rest longer and waits for me to start the conversation. Either way, He is always there when I wake up assuring me the day is under control. Without any vision of my own for the day, I never have a clue how to even start. He lets me know exactly where to start, with some tea, or maybe reading for a bit, sometimes just sitting with Him. The rest of the day is much the same. My life has obligations and responsibilities that must be handled. He helps order each one along with everything in between.

He helps me figure out what I am cooking for meals, in fact my cooking has gotten a hundred times better with Him. With Him helping me in every single step of my day I have confidence in everything I do. I can be adventurous when I listen to His voice because I know He will never steer me wrong. Even if I make a mistake, He will somehow make it a good thing. When His word says that surely He will help me, it doesn't just mean when I am under attack or drowning it means in everything. He wants to help me, to spend time with me, to be as much a part of my life as I will give him. I cannot imagine getting an offer like that from The Great I Am and turning it down. The only reason would be unbelief either in who He is, or unbelief that what He says is true.

Change is hard. Learning to live by His will and not my own has been an unbelievable challenge. There is no way I could have done it on my own. I have Jesus and the Holy Spirit at every turn, giving me wisdom, bolstering my faith, and covering me with peace when I feel like I absolutely can't go on.

I had a dream one night. I was inside an old, dark, sad room. I wasn't particularly sad. I was talking to someone I know. He was laying on a couch and he was looking as he usually does, kind of bitter and hopeless. I saw this little toy go past me on its own out of the door and into the street. I followed the toy into the street, it was headed down by a train that was passing. All of the sudden a huge bunch of red balloons came floating in front of me. They were all tied to white strings and the white strings were bunched together. I grabbed the bundle of strings and a gust of wind came up and blew me into the air. Holding on to the balloons, I was flying high in the sky and fast. I looked down and the ground was a blur. Then more balloons came and surrounded me. They were under and all around me lifting me even higher. Then the balloons started to blow out from under me. There were two men flying along with me. The balloons were starting to blow away. The men kept pushing them back to me and putting them under me. Pretty soon there were just a few balloons left and now I was lower in some dark woods, the men had been pushing the balloons under me so that I came down slowly. Now I was on the ground, and the balloons were gone. That is when I woke up.

God likes to explain things to us. I like when my kids ask me questions and I am able to give them an answer, so does He. So when I woke up asking what that dream meant, He was happy to explain. He had placed a desire in my heart for a husband and a life with him. Then He had recently let that desire walk right past my eyes. He let me see what I had always wanted for my life walk right past me. That dream of what my life could look like was the toy that caught my attention and drew me out of that dark room into the open. Once I was out in the open, the balloons came and carried me away. The balloons were my faith. Once I had walked out into the open, and opened my eyes again to God's goodness and who He is, He was able to send all of these balloons to strengthen my faith. Things that may have gone unnoticed if I hadn't been looking for God in everything. Things I only noticed because I asked Him for them. All of these little ways that God makes Himself evident in our lives showing up every day if only we open our eyes to see. Each one of these thoughts and realizations lifted me higher and closer to God. Each one strengthened my faith.

Each of my days is full of talking with God. One day I asked Him "why does every conversation with you feel so good and so real and then afterwards I remember it like a dream? It fades quickly and tries to leave me." He explained that when I am listening to Him, I am listening with my spirit and not my physical ears. My brain does not hold the information like it would if I were to hear or see with my physical ears or eyes. So it feels more like a dream than reality in memory.

All the little things He was showing me each day and telling me each day were like those balloons. They carried me far away from that place I had wandered to. He went on to explain that as they would start to slip out of my memory, I had angels sent to help keep me afloat pushing them back into my mind constantly. This is the way He chose to rescue me from where I was. All I had to do was open my eyes to Him and then hold on to what He gave me. Even when it would slip out of my grasp, He had sent angels to push it back under me so that I didn't fall.

That left me now in some unfamiliar woods far away from anything I know. Then He gave me a clear picture of Jesus there ready to hold my hand and lead me through the rest of the woods and into the vision He had given me for my life. What could've been a very long journey was just shortened by miles or years or both. God didn't just meet me where I was and tell me to get busy fixing myself. He blew in and picked me up in the most amazing way, carrying me miles beyond what I could've ever imagined.

5:ADONAI

Lord

The heart of the wise is in the house of mourning:
But the heart of fools is in the house of mirth.
Ecclesiastes 7:4 KJV

Then I commended mirth, because a man hath no
better thing under the sun, than to eat, and to drink, and to
be merry: for that shall abide with him of his labor the days
of his life, which God giveth him under the sun.
Ecclesiastes 8:15 KJV

I am no stranger to a good party. I have done a good many things I am not proud of while under the influence, and quite a few I probably shouldn't be proud of, but I can't help but smile when I recall. I also know that in this life there is work to be done. Important work, work that changes people and their eternity. Work to glorify the name of Jesus and to bring people into His presence. There can be nothing more sobering or serious than the stakes that are on the table. The good news is, the war has already been won. God is ultimately in charge and He knows every play, every move, every breath that will be taken. Nothing can happen unless He allows it.

I am part of a war I can not see, I do not understand the rules, and would have no hope of winning on my own. It was a war waged on my behalf. I was fortunate enough to be raised in a home with a foundation in Jesus. I accepted the gift He gave me of grace and mercy as a child. I have been saved and cared for by Him my entire life. It is only recently, I asked God for more.

I don't want to just spend my time on earth scraping by making money to exist until I die. I want to be part of His mighty work on earth. I want to be used to bring glory to Him. I want to arrive in heaven feeling triumphant and confident in my relationship with Jesus Himself. When I asked God for this, He began to pour into me in ways I did not realize were possible. He always gives far more than I expect, and at that point I was asking for and expecting alot.

The knowledge of my ultimate task on this earth changed my heart. Because my heart is with heaven, it is always mourning in some ways, it is always longing for home. When my heart is with heaven and Jesus, the rest of me follows. This is when God began to pour wisdom into me like I had never experienced. My eyes began to see people through His eyes, through a lens of grace. I have been forgiven so much and given so much I do not deserve. That forgiveness and mercy pours out of me. No matter what people are doing, I can not help but offer grace. I know the confusion this life brings. I know how blinding the enemy can be. These are my brothers and sisters in the same unseen war as me, we are on the same side, even if they don't see it.

There is only one thing the bible tells me to fear, and that is God Himself. The fear of God is unlike all other fears though. I know the character of God, I know His mercy, I know the grace He provides. I also know He is holy and just. He does not tolerate sin. This was the unsolvable problem for humanity. Until Jesus solved it. When Jesus took the punishment for my sin, I was made right with God. So now instead of fearing God's inevitable wrath because I can never be spotless, I need only fear falling away from Him. This is the one thing I can control. God promises He will never leave me. He is always merciful and ready to welcome me back with loving arms. When I draw near to Him, He draws even nearer to me. Jesus, having already experienced all the trials and temptations, lovingly guides me out of whatever mess I am in and begins to weed out anything that keeps me distant from Him. So the only fear I should ever have is that I take my eyes off of Jesus. If I keep my eyes on Jesus there is no way I fail.

There is another fear that has crept into Christianity. It is a fear that I have had to deal with. Somewhere a lie crept in that God doesn't want me blessed and happy here on earth. If I expect God to bless me and make me prosperous, then I am only seeking Him for what He can give me. I am human, a fact God is well aware of because He made me. I want to prosper, I want joy and blessing in this life, and that is what God wants for me too. Will it be easy, no. There will be things to overcome, things that draw me closer to God when I start to get pulled away by the desires of my flesh or distractions of this world. Those trials and things to overcome can be celebrated too when I realize that they are pulling me closer to Him.

There is a weight to carry with prosperity, there is an order that must be met in my heart. In order to hold the things God gives me, I have to be able to hold them without letting them consume me. God gave me wine to drink. It is a good thing. However, like all good things it can become a terrible thing if I don't know how to hold it. When I have an aching heart that is lost, hurting, and blind then take a sip of wine I can feel the goodness, warmth, and comfort that it offers. When that is the only thing I use to soothe my aching heart and soul, what was good becomes a poison. The warmth and relaxation of alcohol can not fix heart and soul.

When I am stumbling in the darkness feeling victim to chaos and life and seeking control. I will grab on to anything that eases the pain, or feels like control. Sometimes that can be money, drugs, alcohol, work, other people, nutrition, fitness, or sex. I imagine there are too many things to mention. When I walk through life wounded and hurt with a God-shaped hole in my life, I grasp at whatever feels good in the moment. Then try to turn it into something it can never actually be. Putting anything in the place of God always ends in disaster.

Now for the good news. God doesn't want me to go without food, drink, prosperity, a fulfilling job, a healthy body, a husband, He wants me to have all the goodness He has to offer, things here now and forever. However, I have to be willing to learn how to hold the things He wants to give me or they will destroy me. I have to hold it all with open hands and my eyes on him. This is a big part of the process I have been going through. Letting God order my life. I now understand what it means to have my heart and spirit circumcised. It is sometimes an absolutely crushing and brutal experience. When I am hurting in ways I could've never imagined it only deepens my faith. I have no choice but to absorb and witness the miracle that is transpiring inside of me. A very real pain and change that takes place and could only be the working of almighty God.

I am now desensitized to many of the desires of my heart. Yes, I still want the promises of God. Yes, I still see it all clearly and know it is mine. Now I can tolerate knowing what He has for me in the waiting. Now whether or not I ever receive those desires, I am fulfilled in Him. He is the one who stood with me in the fire. He is the one who has been there all along and promises to be there forever. There is a type of love and bond that can only be forged in that kind of fire. It is a love I would not trade for anything. I sometimes feel as if all of existence could and does slip away and I am standing face to face with Him. He is my Lord, and because He is my all, I am in no danger of holding on to anything else. Things and people can come and go in my life, but He is constant forever. I stand before Him in continual awe and wonder with open hands and a grateful heart ready to give as freely as I receive. There is no fear of loss, there is no wild excitement over gain, because I am whole.

6:YAHWEH-JIREH

The Lord Will Provide

*Delight thyself also in the Lord: and He shall give
thee the desires of thine heart.
Commit thy way unto the Lord; trust also in
Him; and He shall bring it to pass.*
Psalm 37:4-5 KJV

There was an order to discover the true desires of my heart. The world is so full of options today it's hard to distinguish want from need, and desire of the heart from desire of the flesh. God has taken my life and helped me to shed everything that I don't need. It's sort of like an episode of Hoarders, but the things I had to empty out were physical, spiritual, mental, emotional, habits, people, routines, EVERYTHING. He also had me go through my house and clean and empty things physically. He Mr. Miyagi'd me as I was physically emptying my house. He was helping me to mentally, emotionally, and spiritually empty too. With everything pulled out in the open, one room at a time, I was able to get rid of what I no longer needed and put back what I did need in its proper place and in a very tidy and orderly way.

Without all the clutter and mess, I was now able to clearly see what was left. The things left could now be found and used instead of being lost. As I recited Psalm 37:4-5 daily, I would pray "Lord help me to delight in You, help me to commit my way to You, help me to trust in You fully. Thank You for giving me good desires, and thank You for bringing it all to pass."

Each day as I grow closer to Jesus and my relationship

with Him evolves, I delight more and more in Him. I am living a life moment to moment with Him only to light my path. He is my way. I have reached a place in my walk with Him where I am all in. There is no turning back, the boat is gone, it is just He and I on the waves. Without Him I would sink. I am confident that God's word is pure and true. When the word says He will give me the desires of my heart and bring it all to pass, I know I can count on it.

The word is powerful. The more of it that is in my heart, the greater my understanding, and the more power I hold. The knowledge of God's word leaves the enemy helpless. There is no lie of the enemy that won't evaporate into nothing when held up to God's truth. I had another dream one night. I saw myself laying in the bed asleep. There were demons flying at me left and right. My eyes never opened. I would point at one after another and scripture would come out of my mouth and they would burst into nothing. I haven't had a bad night's sleep in a while now. I sleep more peacefully now than I ever have. If I wake up in the night it is to have a chat with Jesus until I fall back asleep, and that is always worth waking up for.

Jesus finished everything on the cross. I only have to be willing to accept what He offers to me. One morning, I had a house full of sleeping girls, as I usually do. I woke up and asked Jesus what I should start with today. He told me to go to the store and get stuff to make biscuits and gravy. So I hopped in the car, grabbed the food and came back to start cooking. When I got back, He said "we are going to cook all twenty biscuits", I started to argue in my head thinking we will never eat all twenty in a morning. So I talked myself into putting thirteen on a cookie sheet. Why I needed to put seven less, I do not know. Then He says to me, "We aren't just making sausage gravy, let's make the chocolate gravy you used to have at Laticia's house when you were a kid too." I hadn't made that in years, and only maybe twice ever, but I said Ok. I looked up the recipe and started to get things together. Then He said "put the rest of the biscuits in the oven, Andrea." So I got out another cookie sheet and put in the last seven biscuits.

It wasn't long before one of the girls came out and started talking with me. It was Sophie's best friend, Amya. She stayed in the kitchen and talked to me while I was making both gravies but wandered off to take a shower towards the end. As I finished both pans of gravy and pulled the last biscuits out of the oven, I was now staring at a massive breakfast and no one in the house was awake except for Amya and I. Amya was still in the shower, so it was just me.

God said "It's kind of annoying isn't it. You've got all this good food ready to be eaten and no one is awake to eat it." I started to see where this was going. He said, "Go wake everyone up." So I went bedroom to bedroom waking everyone up. Eventually everyone stumbled out to the table to eat. Then like a bunch of zombies they were all just sitting there staring at their food. God said "eat." So I started to eat, and about the time they saw me start in on the biscuit with chocolate gravy, everyone else started to eat. God then said "I have all of these wonderful things to give and everyone is asleep. I need you to wake them up. Some people are already at the table but they are afraid to eat. You are going to eat and show them how good it is."

Then out came Amya. She made herself a biscuit with chocolate gravy, and she couldn't stop talking about how great it was. God said "It always tastes better when you watch me make it for you." Then I looked back at the giant pan of leftover biscuits. He said "there is more than enough for everyone."

7:EL-BERITH

God of the Covenant

"For verily I say unto you, that whosoever shall say unto this mountain, Be thou removed, and be thou cast into the sea; and shall not doubt in his heart, but shall believe that those things which he saith shall come to pass; he shall have whatsoever he saith. Therefore I say unto you, what things so ever ye desire, when ye pray, believe that ye receive them, and ye shall have them. And when ye stand praying, forgive, if ye have ought against any: that your Father also which is in heaven may forgive you your trespasses. But if ye do not forgive, neither will your Father which is in heaven forgive you your trespasses.
Mark 11:23-26 KJV

I have a dog named Gracie. She is a blue nosed pit bull that wandered out of the woods near my grandmother's house when she was just a puppy and covered in ticks. She is the most friendly and social dog you will ever meet. She knows everyone in the neighborhood and even has a best friend named Penny that lives a few houses down the road. She is a very well behaved dog, she doesn't bark much, doesn't jump on people or chew up what she's not supposed to, but she does like to run off and visit the neighbors without permission.

One morning while I was outside with her, waiting for her to finish her business, a large group of cyclists came up the road. I could see the longing on her face. She looked at me then looked at them, then started to bolt. I yelled her name. She froze and looked at me again. She usually stops if she sees that I can see her still, if she is behind a tree or something she will pretend she never heard me. The cyclists were still rolling past. I saw her head turn again and again as she bolted. I yelled her name again and she froze. This time I walked down the deck steps toward her until she started walking toward me and gave up on the cyclists.

I had just been having a conversation with God that morning about getting distracted. At that time God still had me in a full bubble, kids were busy with camps and summer things, and it was just He and I all day everyday. I had been worried that when life returned to full swing, I would lose Him in the distractions and get off the path He had set me on. As I was walking Gracie back in the house, He said "You would've kept calling Gracie's name until she listened wouldn't you? And even if she took off down the road, you know exactly where to get her from. You would've gone and picked her up and brought her home wouldn't you?"

Of course I would.

"Well don't you think I will keep calling your name until I get your attention? Don't you know that even if you wander off, I know where to come get you?"

I have no context, no words, no experience that comes close to capturing the way God feels about me. The way Jesus feels about me. The way the Holy Spirit moves in my life. He reminds me that the way I love my kids, my dog, or even an imaginary ant, are only faint and blurry reflections of the pure love that He is. He gives us these feelings and experiences to show us more of Himself. I long for the day when I am ready to see Him face to face, but until that time, every piece of His character that is revealed keeps me in awe.

He longs to be with me, to give me good things, to let me know Him and be known. He wants me whole and full of the power and dominion I was created to hold over the earth. I was given free will. Not only do I have the power to accept the salvation that Jesus offers, but I have the choice to ask for more. Once I have accepted salvation from Jesus I am saved. God wants to give me more. He wants me to be wise and take the things He is offering me here on this earth, and in this life. He wants to show me how to use them to bring glory to the kingdom.

In bringing glory to the kingdom, I also store up treasures in heaven. What better way to spend this life than working to bring people to Jesus? It gives my life meaning now and forever. This is where true joy and happiness and peace lie. I know that the work I am doing here and now pleases God, glorifies my Savior, and helps to bring more of my brothers and sisters into eternal glory with me.

If anyone can think of a more satisfying or fulfilling way to live your life, I would love to hear about it. God doesn't promise earthly pleasures, and an easy life. He does promise; provision, purpose, peace, joy, and love. He also promises to put desires in my heart, so that the things I want are from Him, and therefore able to be received. All I have to do is ask. When I am confident that what I am asking for is in the will of God, then I approach Him with even more boldness.

As I would recite Mark 11:23-26 I would also pray confidently "God give me the wisdom to know which mountains to move, and the faith to move them. Thank you for giving me the desires of my heart and showing me how to believe so that I may receive them. If I have any unforgiveness in my heart, show me, and then help me to forgive." This is a prayer that is backed by the word of God. I could pray boldly, knowing God would deliver.

People act like it is sinful or evil to want the good things of this life. To want prosperity and blessing here and now too. It is not. I know that God will happily bless me so much that it pours out of me and into the lives of everyone around me. He has to prepare me for it first though. The process is wild and painful, but also exciting and fulfilling. It has drawn me closer to Jesus than I ever imagined possible. I would do it a million times over without hesitation. God never disappoints.

God has been blessing his chosen people since the beginning. He wants to give me all of the good things He has prepared for me. Jesus makes me able to confidently accept everything. There is an order that things must be done in, and God's timing is not mine, but He wants to bless me with it all.

There is plenty to go around. I have to keep Jesus first. He shows me how to lay it all down at the foot of the cross. This sounds easy but I assure you it would be impossible without Jesus and the Holy Spirit.

God doesn't change, He is outside of time. The promises He made in the beginning are as true today as they were the day He spoke them. I have chosen to accept every good thing He is offering me. I gratefully accept things He offers now in this life and those things He offers for eternity. I don't want to waste one more second at the table not eating what God has so lovingly prepared for me.

8:YAHWEH-NISSI

The Lord Our Banner

For though we walk in the flesh, we do not war after the flesh;
For the weapons of our warfare are not carnal, but mighty through God to
the pulling down of strongholds; Casting down imaginations, and every
high thing that exalteth itself against the knowledge of God, and bringing
into captivity every thought to the obedience of Christ. And having in a
readiness to revenge all disobedience, when your obedience is fulfilled.
II Corinthians 10:3-6 KJV

It is hard to imagine fighting a war I can not see. A war that for the most part takes place inside my heart and mind. If war is being waged in my heart and mind, then the things that take place inside them must be where my attention is focused. When God's word tells me I am at war, it isn't to make me feel powerless or afraid. It is in fact just the opposite. He is reminding me that I am powerful. With Him I have nothing to fear. I am made aware of what is taking place so that I can claim the victory with Him. Jesus has paid the price for my sins, my soul is safe in Him. As I walk through this life, I will be in the middle of a war. It is fought with God and through God. There is one way to be victorious in this life and that is through Him.

Our enemy is confusion, lies, fear, anger, bitterness, lust, greed, he is the pure form of all that seeks to devour us from the inside out. Without God we are easily seduced or wounded or more likely both. We give him stronghold after stronghold without ever realizing what we have done. Before we know it our lives are not our own. We are walking in a deep rut. We don't know how we made it but we know it's not what we were made for. Our lives become a prison. We soon find ourselves back in Egypt, slaves.

I took the airpods out of my ears one day, they had been in most all the day, every day. I used music to motivate me through my day, or so I thought. When I took them out, it was uncomfortable for a while. At first, it felt like my energy and focus were gone. Then I realized it was just that my thoughts could actually develop in my head without the constant noise in my ears. Yes, I can think and listen to music at the same time, but it's not the same kind of thinking that occurs in stillness and silence. No, my life is rarely actually still or silent. In fact it is well after midnight now and someone is rattling around in a bathroom currently. There is rarely complete stillness in life, when you find it revel in it. However, I had become accustomed to constant sensory input. I was constantly feeding my eyes and ears something, and thinking about what I would feed my face next. Being present in the moment without any kind of external input was not something I knew how to do.

There is a quote I love by C.S. Lewis "The present is the point at which time touches eternity." I am currently stuck inside of time. I am an eternal being, I have eternity written in my heart, I long for it. Right now I must live moment by moment. This present moment is the only way I have to touch eternity, to feel it, or change it. I was living in such a way and I do not believe it was by accident, that every single moment of the present was consumed by either music, video, rushing to the next obligation, worrying about the future, or thinking about the past.

When I think of all of the time that was lost to those things it feels like an unbearable tragedy. God is beyond loving and merciful and He has no limitations. I woke up and saw myself in chains and a slave to a million different habits, worries, and wants. In that very moment of time that I called to Him for help, everything changed. Because God lives outside of time, even the past can be changed by the action you take in the present. Eternity goes both backward and forward. When the decision is made to accept what God is offering you, God makes all the mistakes of the past into a blessing for the future. He turns what the Devil meant for evil into something so good.

Often it seems that the bigger the hurt, the deeper the wound, the more good that God is able to do with it. God is a God who restores and when He restores He doesn't just put things back the way they were before they got broken. He makes it into something better than it ever could've been.

I do not know how to move in a war I can't see. God does. I can not change the past. God can. I cannot navigate the course to the future I desire. God will. I need only to listen to His voice and act in obedience. Over the course of the last few months my life has been completely deconstructed in such a way that everything I do now is an act of obedience. I involve Him in every single decision. Because He is involved, everything I do is done with confidence and free from worry.

One evening as I was laying down talking to Him. He started explaining how my obedience in every moment blossoms out into blessings that spin out into eternity. He told me to think of a fractal. It is a repeating pattern that goes down infinitely small and continues out infinitely large. They are found everywhere in nature. He said that what I do in the present moment creates a sort of pattern. This pattern continues down infinitely small inside of me, and continues out infinitely large into the world around me. Not only does it do that, but it goes back into time, and forward into the future, and then in sort of the same way in all of these other dimensions and directions that I can not even begin to fathom. When I sin, that is what is being replicated in all those ways. Jesus died for me and shed his blood to cover those patterns of sin. I can stand before God even as a sinner, because his blood covers the patterns I created in sin. I am seen as spotless and clean.

However, when I act in obedience and in ways that are pleasing to God in the present, I create these beautiful patterns that spiral out in all the same ways. They travel inside of me replicating infinitely small and consuming. They travel out of me replicating infinitely large, reaching even heaven. They go into my past, then go into my future and again into so many other dimensions and directions I can not fathom.

So in every moment, I have a choice. I have already accepted Jesus, I am clean and I am able to stand before God. Now the choice is, do I continue to sin and change nothing, or do I act in obedience and let my life be an act of worship. Creating endless patterns of beauty, like a sweet fragrance, and a song, and the most beautiful blooming flowers that spiral out into eternity and deep into myself changing me and everything around me for the better. I choose to worship in obedience in every single moment that I can. God is faithful. When I please Him, I feel His joy, His love and His presence abound. There is nothing more precious in this life that I have ever experienced.

I am fully aware that my mind is a battlefield, this does not cause me to worry. Jesus is the name above all names, and He says I am His. I need only keep my eyes on Him and claim the victory He has already won.

9: EL
God (Mighty, strong, prominent)

*What would have become of me had I not believed that I
would see the Lord's goodness in the land of the living! Wait
and hope for and expect the Lord; be brave and of good
courage and let your heart be stout and enduring.*
Psalm 27:13-14 AMP

What does it mean to wait? This has been the hardest
part for me, the waiting. I'm good at following orders and doing
whatever task is set out before me. When God tells me to wait,
this is where it gets really hard for me. It is the opposite of
what you would think. God giving the order to go somewhere,
do something, talk to someone, that would logically be the hard
part. Just sit with Me, know that I am God, and trust Me would
seem easy in comparison. This sitting, this waiting, is where
the trust is built though. This is the place where I am forced
to let go of any shred of control I cling to. Looking around and
seeing the life I have always known just falling away, every sense
I've ever been taught to trust screaming at me that I am losing
everything, and doing nothing. There is no way to understand
this process, other than to live through it.

It would not be possible without the Holy Spirit and Jesus.
The very fact that I have more peace and joy than I have ever felt
in the midst of what looks like my entire life falling away must
be supernatural. Everything that ever made me feel like I had
some form of control is gone. One by one everything in my life
has been handed over to Him. In the process of cleaning out my

house we cleaned out my life. Everything we would come to, a question would be asked "Do you want to handle this, or Do you want to give it to me?" The answer is always "Please take it!"

Some things were easier to hand over than others. Areas where I was obviously struggling and needed rescue were easier to hand over. It is the few areas in my life where I felt I was doing well that were the hardest to hand over. Those were the places where I still held the illusion of control. I would stop long enough to answer the question, Can God most definitely do this better than me? The answer is always a resounding yes. This is where some will try to tell me, I'm seeking the things of the world because I ask for more with my health, my hair, my kids, my finances, my everything. If God asks if I want Him to help in every area of my life, why would I ever say no? That seems like the real sin to me. Saying no to God, because of some proud and pious notion that as a christian I must suffer through this life. He wants to help. I am going to let Him.

People often say, "Well God doesn't always give you prosperity, He uses people who are humble, poor people that still give freely, not everyone can have those kinds of blessings." I can only speak of my personal experience with God, and what I have read in His word. I know what He has spoken to me and I know what He has offered me. He told me there would be a process to get to the things I desire, and it would be difficult. He also told me, it is done. He gave me the yes. I believe He wants to give a yes to everyone who asks. He wants me to believe fully that because of what Jesus did for me, nothing is off limits. I can stand freely before the throne of grace and ask for whatever desire He puts in my heart. I need to be confident in the desires of my heart first. This is done by seeking Jesus first and then allowing Him to place the desires in my heart.

God never disappoints. He put desires in my heart that are far beyond anything I could have ever dreamed for myself. This is where my faith in the work of the cross and foundation in the word are crucial. The Devil immediately painted a picture of me as greedy and proud and undeserving. He isn't wrong. I am sure

I am all of those things, but because of the cross God sees me as perfect and blameless. Sorry Devil, the cross is more powerful than anything you say or anything I have done. So I still stand before the throne of God with open hands smiling.

The things God has promised He will do. He doesn't give me everything until it has all been prepared, and I am prepared to hold it. He isn't going to give me what will crush me. He makes me strong enough to hold whatever He gives me.

My boldness comes not from myself but from the cross. God wants me blessed and able to bless others. I have to be obedient, and to trust Him though in order to hold the blessings He wants to give me. I have to learn to trust Him fully, and to keep my eyes on Him no matter what life looks like. The weight of prosperity and blessing is heavy. It will pull me away from God if I haven't built my foundation solely on Him. Saying no to what God has offered me would be saying, I do not have faith that He can do it, or I do not believe that the cross made me able to receive it, or both. I never want to say no to God. I want to come to Him trusting that there is nothing He can not do. I stand before Him made whole and perfect by the work of the cross. I trust that every part of me that needs work, He will finish. I know that I can do all things because He is with me.

So as I wait, I am confident that the waiting is part of the work. In being still, and knowing He is God, I am building trust. What the world would tell me is doing nothing, might be the most important work of all. He does some of His best work when I am still with my eyes focused only on Him.

10:ELOHIM
God (more than two, mighty, strong, creator)

Behold, O God our Shield, and look upon the face of thine anointed.
For a day in Thy courts is better than a thousand. I had rather be
a doorkeeper in the house of my God, than to dwell in the tents of
wickedness. For the Lord God is a sun and shield: the Lord will give
grace and glory: No good thing will He withhold from them that walk
uprightly. O Lord of hosts, Blessed is the man that trusteth in Thee.
Psalm 84:9-12 KJV

Every time I think I have gone as deep as I can go with God, He takes me deeper. There is a joy, a peace, a hope and a love that never stop growing in me. Everytime I am sure there can be nothing more, nothing better, God shows me there is. There is a closeness I have developed with God. I can not imagine that too many people talk to God all day long about everything. If they did, the world would be a very different place. I went from locked out of my own head with music, instagram reels, business, television, workouts, and any other distraction at hand, to living for the conversation in my head. My entire world changed in what seemed like an instant.

Once I recognized that God is with me, always, and wants to talk, why would I ever want to do anything else. Everything else pales in comparison. One night as I was drifting off to sleep I had another one of those odd thoughts drift through my brain. This one was a little more odd than usual. What if you put a baby in a dolphin to finish gestating? Weird, I know. But the weird stuff is usually the best. Ok let's think this through. Well if you put a human baby in a dolphin to gestate, the problem will be it's going to be born under water. You will need to make it able to breathe underwater, or teach it to swim really quick, or pull it out of the water all together. Ok now imagine I am in the dolphin's belly, I am a baby dolphin about to be born. I have never thought about it but I suppose a baby dolphin has to get to the surface to breathe pretty soon after being born. Then I began to think about how dolphins live in two different worlds. The really live under the water, but yet they have to come up to breathe.

God then began to explain to me that I am like that little dolphin. I came up to breathe the spiritual air, and now I don't want to put my head back in the water. I have been treading water with my head up talking to him and breathing in the air. Once I realized what was above the water, I didn't want to go back down in it. But it is incredibly tiring treading water for very long and I am not seeing all that the water has to offer. It is not where I am meant to stay. He is going to teach me how to be a dolphin and live in both worlds at the same time. Breathing Him in like air but also swimming through the world at the same time. I will be like a dolphin swimming and playing and coming up to be with Him as often as I breathe. This metaphor is one that I could never have come up with in a million years, especially not as I was lying in bed falling asleep. It is the way God speaks His truth so often.

I have found a joy in Him that I did not know was possible. He answered my prayer to help me delight in him. I now delight so much that it is hard to like anything else. That was a problem, but not for God. He just lets me know we are doing it together. Even though my eyes might go down into the water for a minute while I am focused on what I am doing in life. He is right there with me still. I need only pause for a breathe and think of Him and He responds. He will never let me get lost in my life.

Sleep is a strange thing. I often hear Him most clearly right on waking when my mind is still empty and fresh, or sometimes as my mind is shutting down and I am beginning to drift. There have been many days when God was pouring so much information into me, we would talk all day long, and by the end of the day my brain and body felt like it couldn't think another thought. I suppose I was building faith by walking in the spirit all day. Like any other form of vigorous exercise, it made me incredibly tired.

Somewhere around one or two a.m. I would wake up most nights to that gentle coaxing from the Holy Spirit, and Jesus right there whispering "Hey wake up, sit up and turn on the light, I've got something to tell you, it will be worth it." As tired as I would be I would smile. The Lord himself was waking me up eager to share things with me how could I not smile, and He never disappointed me it was always so so worth waking up. I would wake up and sometimes He would tell me to start reading my bible and that would turn into a conversation, sometimes it would just be conversation.

I had always had sleep issues ever since I was a kid. It would frustrate me when I couldn't sleep, which in turn made it almost impossible to sleep because my frustration would just build. God is the ultimate multitasker though. While He was waking me up to talk with me He was also teaching me that waking up at night doesn't have to frustrate me. In fact, laying in bed tired is probably my favorite thing to do now, because I know He is there to talk with me until I eventually drift off to sleep. Then if I do wake up in the middle of the night I wake up assuming it's Him wanting to talk so it is more to look forward to. So with the knowledge that He gave me in those conversations, came a release from the frustration that sleep had always brought me. God is so good.

Now when I wake in the night, it's never in a panic thinking about things that need to be done, mistakes I've made, or some random anxiety or fear. Instead I wake with a smile and a Hello because I know Who is right there with me. There is nowhere I would rather be than with Him, and He is always with me. So wherever I am is exactly where I want to be.

11:EL SHADDAI

God Almighty

I will lift up mine eyes unto the hills, from whence cometh my help.
My help cometh from the Lord, which made heaven and earth.
He will not suffer thy foot to be moved: He that
keepeth thee will not slumber.
Behold he that keepeth Israel shall neither slumber nor sleep.
The Lord is thy keeper: the Lord is thy shade upon thy right hand.
The sun shall not smite thee by day, nor the moon by night.
The Lord shall preserve thee from all evil: he shall preserve
thy soul. The Lord shall preserve thy going out and thy
coming in from this time forth and even forevermore.
Psalm 121 KJV

There is one thing that makes listening for God really difficult. He is not the only voice that enters my thoughts. When I began listening to Him, it was because I heard His voice and my spirit recognized it instantly. One of those things where when you know you know. It was Him, there was no doubt in me. God doesn't always speak to me like that, so clearly and loudly and encased in emotion. More often than not, I had to slowly discern that it was indeed Him by what He was saying.

My voice is also in there, it is usually more like a train of thought that frequently runs off the track. The fact that God is a three in one kind of deal, is something my mind still struggles to wrap around. Somedays I feel like I understand it a little better than others. There are different ways in which He communicates to me. The logistics of it are something I am not privy to.

Then there is another voice, this one changes but usually brings about the same feelings eventually. This is the voice of the enemy. Either I have gotten better at silencing it, or God has him on low volume at the moment. Whatever the case, I am grateful. For awhile, I tried to figure out the rules to how the enemy operated. Could he use scripture, could he make me feel good, just different ways to try and discern quickly. The answer to that question is he has no rules he plays by. He will do anything in his power to deceive, confuse, and steal whatever joy and peace he can from me.

The good news is Jesus has authority over him. There is nothing he can do that Jesus can't undo. When I am following Jesus closely and listening to him, there is nothing the enemy can do to me unless God allows it. The only reason God might allow the enemy to come against me in some way, is because He knows I can handle it and He will turn it into good for me. I am far from being able to understand or explain the mysteries of why God allows what He does. I can tell you from my personal experience in the fire and with the attacks of the enemy. God has showed me in every instance how He used it for my good. It strengthened me in a way that only opposition and trial could. I also know that while the devil and his demons are very real, the best thing I can do is not think about them or speak about them more than I need to. They are real, they are present but they are powerless in the shadow of my God. So I remember Who is in charge.

When a thought in my head starts to lead me in a direction I know is not from God, I picture it like a tiny weed trying to sprout and I pluck it and toss it out of my mind. Anytime the thought is leading toward fear, anger, doubt in God, any sin or direction that is obviously opposed to what God wants for me according to his word, I know it needs to go. Sometimes I stop for a minute and think about it and am quickly able to see that it is founded usually in a lie or fear or doubt. The more I have practiced plucking these thoughts the easier it has gotten.

When I am speaking with God, I often look up. I know that isn't really where He is, He is in me and around me and everywhere, but it is now like a switch I have installed in my brain. When my eyes look up in that way, it reminds me He is there. My brain automatically starts a conversation with Him. It feels like glancing at my best friend acknowledging that they are there seeing this with me.

Being reminded He is always with me is a priceless treasure. The Maker of heaven and earth, is my help, my keeper. He promises to not let my foot be moved. This is scripture I stand on, and use against the lies of the enemy often. When the thoughts in my head get loud, and they are trying to convince me that I am a fool, or crazy, lost, and headed for disaster. I remember Who my trust is in. My trust is in the Lord. He does not sleep. He will not let my foot be moved. He won't let me be harmed day or night. He keeps me from evil. He even keeps everything I do. My trust is in him, seeking Him and listening to Him in every way I can. I know that He has me covered, so I will not fall into worry and doubt.

12:YAHWEH-ROPHE
The Lord Who Heals, Mends, Repairs

O sing unto the Lord a new song; for He
hath done marvelous things:
His right hand, and His holy arm, hath gotten Him the victory.
Psalms 98:1 KJV

On a recent trip to the store, I noticed a man who was struggling to walk. He pushed his cart out of the door and came over to a nice truck next to me. I could tell every step, every move, every breath was causing him pain. He was fighting to walk, to push a cart, then to lift one thing at a time into the passenger seat. I don't know what was in his bags, but I noticed he had a lot of Soda. I couldn't help but feel like he had given up on ever feeling better. I don't know what that man had been through, and dealt with in his life to get him to that point. I do know there is a God that loves him dearly. I do know that being trapped in a body that feels more like a torture chamber is not where He wants him.

It is so easy to trade all the goodness He has given me for one little fleeting pleasure at a time. Those pleasures never satisfy, they always demand more more more, and they leave me feeling worse.

I love to eat. I always have. In fact, I have been told I eat like I've been to prison, or like the food is trying to run off my plate. God gave me food to enjoy, He wants me to enjoy it. Like any good thing God gives me, food can be turned into something it shouldn't be. When food is taking the place of God, it will turn to poison. It can not fix my loneliness, my broken heart, ease my boredom, or my sense of purposelessness.

The enemy has turned food into something it shouldn't be. Food was intended to nourish my body. God is good and wants me to experience pleasure and joy. He made food of all different types and made it something I could delight in. The pleasure of sharing a meal when I am hungry is a wonderful thing, a gift from God. When I spend all day snacking on things that taste good for a second and then immediately leave me both feeling sick and somehow wanting more, I never even get to experience a hungry state. There is a pleasure in food that comes only when I am actually hungry. It is very easy in the world now to go my whole life and never experience real hunger. I am far from rich, in fact at this point in my life I pray before every dollar I spend. It would be a tragedy to go my whole life never knowing how food tasted when I was really hungry.

There is a joy in self denial. I have been learning to slow down with my food. The first thing God had me do was take my food to the table. I had become very bad about sitting in front of the TV with my food. He showed me that I wasn't even enjoying the food the way it was meant to be enjoyed when I did that. It was just like a mass sensory dump. Food was being shoveled into my mouth while information was being shoveled into my eyes and ears. When I sit at the table and think about what I am eating, I can actually enjoy the food. I felt like I was enjoying the food in front of the TV, but trust me it was so much better once I learned to sit and think about what I was eating. I could actually remember the experience of eating, and have real meaningful conversation with my kids, or with God.

God made all types of food, He wants me to enjoy them all. He wants me to actually enjoy them though, not just mindlessly gobble without thinking. There are other ways He has helped me in my relationship with food. I have always eaten everything on my plate. Well maybe not always, but for the most part if it was on my plate, I ate it. I think maybe it's because I know it always made my grandmother so happy to see I had finished my food. Anyway, this had made me eat like I was in a race. One day God told me, "I want you to just leave a little bit on your plate everytime you eat. Just remember you are doing it for me. You can get seconds if you want, but before you put your plate away there should be some food to scrape off left." This changed the way I eat completely. Somehow knowing that I wasn't going to devour everything on my plate slowed me down. As I would see my food start to dwindle I would slow down and start thinking about what I would leave on my plate. This made me enjoy the last bites even more than the first somehow. I knew I wouldn't eat it all, it wasn't a chore to be completed, it was something to slow down and savor.

When I begin to let God into every part of my life, He begins to heal every part of my life, every part of me. He fixes my broken ways of thinking, my broken heart, and my body. I see so many people every day that just look like prisoners in their own bodies. It breaks my heart. What feels impossible, God can do so easily. I have watched Him change me one conversation at a time. It is the most fascinating, exciting, miraculous thing I have ever experienced. He is so loving in the way He heals. He never told me I was making mistakes, He showed me how and why things were going the way they were and then taught me a better way.

13: YAHWEH-SHALOM

The Lord Our Peace

He delighteth not in the strength of the horse: He
taketh not pleasure in the legs of a man.
The Lord taketh pleasure in them that fear Him,
in those that hope in His mercy.
Psalm 147:10-11 KJV

My life was so overwhelming for a very long time. I had created routines and habits to try and give myself some sense of control. One day I realized that those habits and routines had created a very deep rut that I was circling, one that seemed to get deeper with every lap around. Those routines were all I looked forward to each day. They really became all I could see for the day. I had no vision, no hope of any real change each day. Sure, some days would have an extra birthday party or dinner, or different characters, but really it was the same day over and over again for the most part. No wonder I was bored with life, desperately trying to fill it with whatever temporary relief was at hand.

I had always heard routine and structure gives you a sense of peace and makes life less chaotic. In fact, I had always felt like what my life needed was more structure. I thought if only I could be better with doing things at a certain time each day, I could fit it all in and it would make me feel better. I am realizing now that what I needed was the exact opposite. I had created a prison out of my day.

In the deconstruction of each day God took those bars down one at a time. He gave me freedom that I didn't even realize I had lost. Had I just given up all my routines on my own, I would've been completely lost and helpless. I wouldn't have known which way to move. I was not on my own. He was right there leading me through each step of the day. Many days He would tell me "Don't try and figure out where this day is going, you won't be able to, and you don't need to. Just trust me and let's go one step at a time." This is the complete opposite of the life I had been leading. There is no boredom when each step is being led by God Almighty. He introduced me to life that can be an adventure every single moment of every single day.

One day in the waiting, as I was doing dishes, I was talking with God. I am talking with God more often than not these days and it is the best part of my life. Anyway, the waiting is hard. I know things are coming, really really good things. There I am, though doing the dishes and talking to God. I am talking about how excited I am for the future and I can't wait to get there and have all these wonderful adventures. Very gently and almost with a half smile, this is one of those things I just feel I never see, he says "You know Andrea, this is the good part too." This warmth just flooded me and I felt a huge smile spread across my face. I can't think of one single second with Him that hasn't been the good part. Even in the tears and pain, there are parts I would not trade for anything.

There is a way that He manages to put together every piece of my life, my heart, my mind, my soul, everything, and it just fits so perfectly. He makes me whole. Then He teaches me how to listen to Him, follow Him, and walk with Him. When I am whole and walking in step with Him I have a peace and a joy that is indescribable.

14:YAHWEH-ELOHIM

Lord God

Arise, shine; for thy light is come, and the glory
of the Lord is risen upon thee.
For, behold, the darkness shall cover the earth,
and gross darkness the people:
But the Lord shall arise upon thee, and His glory shall be seen upon thee.
Isaiah 60:1-2 KJV

There was one night I was sleeping, and I woke just enough to feel myself laying in bed and the room was dark. Maybe I was still in a dream, I don't know. I remember it like it was real, like I saw it with my eyes. Isaiah 60:1-2 went through my mind. Though my room was dark I could see like it was light. It wasn't like daylight or a light in the house. I could just see clearly as though everything had been lit up. Then I saw outside in my back yard and it was dark, the moon was out and bright. There was a light though coming from somewhere, I could see everything as clearly as if it was daytime even in the darkness. Then I could almost see myself laying in bed, and I felt the light, the warmth, spreading across me and shining on me. It was like I was glowing.

I believe in the power of God's word. I believe in the power of the Holy Spirit to light passages up in my heart and in my spirit. One of the biggest attacks the enemy has used against me is to tell me I'm being prideful or greedy or delusional or all of those. That to claim such good things over myself is a sin. God on the other hand pours love and praise out to me. He always lavishes me with kindness and goodness. I need only remember that anything good I have, or am comes from Him.

In the writing of this book, the enemy has tried over and over again to convince me that God would never use me, that I am being proud or vain. That I'm boasting and expecting things I shouldn't. Pride is the big one. We all know that's what got the devil in trouble in the first place.

Sometimes God gives me an unspeakable word. A word to say in my head. It is not a word I've ever heard. When I repeat it in my head and meditate on it, its meaning is revealed to me. I could come up with synonyms for the word, but they would not fully capture the meaning it carries. Because the Devil had been accusing me of pride lately, God gave me a new word last night.

Before when He has given me the word, He has given me a sort of synonym first to help me understand what the word is. This time He just gave me the word and told me to say the word a few times in my head and clear my thoughts. At first as I was saying the word, I felt like I was seeing an eye. So then I was trying to figure out what it had to do with an eye. Like He has so many times before, He told me to stop trying to figure it out and just listen. When I stopped trying and just listened I could see that what I thought was an eye was one of the spots on a peacock's feathers. Immediately, a voice in my head starts screaming run, run, this is the devil trying to convince you that pride is good, don't be a proud peacock, you will end up in flames. At first, I felt panic. Then I remembered who wanted me to panic. I remembered God never makes me feel that way. God whispered gently "just keep thinking about the word." He has also taught me to not be afraid of my thoughts. I can confidently follow them until I see where they are going and then decide what to do with them. So I kept thinking. I could now see a beautiful peacock with its feathers all fanned out.

God asked me "Is it a sin that the peacock be seen, is it a sin that he shows the feathers I created for him." Of course it's not a sin. God has created lots of beautiful things. He created them to be seen not to be hidden. The peacock doesn't boast that he created the feathers himself. He just shows them. As long as what we are displaying points back to the One who created it, it is not a sin. It is in fact a way of praising God. The tragedy would be if the peacock hid himself so that no one could ever see God's beautiful work.

15:YAHWEH-SHAMMAH

The Lord is there

That the God of our Lord Jesus Christ, the Father of Glory,
may give to you the spirit of wisdom and
revelation in the knowledge of Him,
the eyes of your understanding being enlightened;
that you may know what is the hope of His calling, what are the riches
of the glory of His inheritance in the saints, and what is the exceeding
greatness of His power to us-ward who believe, according to the working
of His mighty power which He worked in Christ when He raised Him from
the dead and seated Him at His own right hand in the heavenly places,
far above all power and principality and might and dominion, and every
name that is named, not only in this age but in that which is to come.
Ephesians 1:17-21 KJV

This is my prayer. That God...will give you spiritual
wisdom and the insight to know more of him:
That you may receive that inner illumination of the spirit which will
make you realize how great is the hope to which he is calling you and
how tremendous is the power available to us who believe in God.
Ephesians 1:17-19 NKJV

When I had reached a dead end in life, God said "you made it!". When I couldn't see which way to go, He said "I'll show you!". There is an open mindedness, and a searching that took place when I finally realized I could not go any further on my own. I don't know how I made it 44 years without him. The answer I suppose is that I didn't. He was there opening doors, closing doors, nudging me, and then rescuing me the whole time. Even when I had my eyes down at the ground scared to look up, He still had His eyes on me. He had His eyes on me before the beginning of everything. I can say those things with belief now. When I stop and weigh the gravity of those statements, time stands still, everything that is not Him falls away. I am standing in a perfect place.

I have been called by the Father, rescued by the Savior, and I am guided by the Holy Spirit. My life has a purpose and a calling that I can not even begin to fathom. He has called me to be a part of something so powerful words can not describe. I asked to be given a purpose, for Him to take my life and make it mean something, to use my life for His glory in the most spectacular way possible, whatever that may look like to me. Since that day He has been pouring into me. He has been refining me. He has invited me into a family full of wonder and adventure and calling.

Since this process got started, my dreams have taken on a life of their own. They have meaning, sometimes that meaning is explained to me. One night I dreamt I was dog sitting for some cousins at an Aunt's house. The dog ran off down the block while I was outside, so I followed it down the road. I came to a large complex of buildings and a big structure that looked like a temple. I remember feeling like it was some sort of very religious group that most certainly did not want me near. I saw the dog run in. I saw lots of people in religious garb. Some were dressed like Hacedic Jews, some looked like they were Pentacostal, I don't know that the clothes mattered but I know I felt like they were part of something that I was not, and I most likely did not want to be. I knew I had to go in and get the dog but I did not want to, I was sure they were going to be angry and chase me out. I went in anyway. As I walked on the grounds things started to look different. I saw people doing acrobatics, blowing fire and dressed like entertainers in the circus. I kept going and I saw water slides and what looked like regular people riding down the slides. Some of them were laughing and having fun, and some looked like they were holding on for dear life.

Then I saw what looked like training grounds, people were doing all kinds of obstacle courses and learning to climb through and over things and complete challenges. It all looked incredible. I wanted to be a part of it. I met a man who invited me to join them. I did. Then I remembered the dog. That is when I woke up.

What I had thought was a bunch of crazy religious people were actually part of the most amazing thing I had ever seen. They were all different, they looked different and had different things they were doing but they were all part of the same thing. They were all operating in their own areas but under the same purpose. I knew that was where I wanted to be. It made the rest of the world fade into nothingness. Like a dull gray dream I did not want to return to.

16:PALET

Deliverer

But they that wait upon the Lord shall renew their strength;
they shall mount up with wings as eagles;
they shall run, and not be weary; and they shall walk, and not faint.
Isaiah 40:31 KJV

Here is that word again "wait". One of the hardest things I have ever done is to wait. It's tiring, it can feel confusing, frustrating, and it makes me realize how powerless I am. To wait on the Lord, means to trust that He is doing something. If you are waiting then that means you are expecting something. There is a helplessness in waiting. Right before I started this chapter God gave me another word. This time I saw a dandelion, with all of its seeds ready to blow away in the wind. I am like a dandelion seed and God is the wind. He knows what is inside me. He knows what kind of fruit and flower I will bear. So He knows where He will put me. If I let myself become full of sin and bitterness He might blow me over a swamp or onto some rocks or somewhere out of sight until I can grow again. Next time producing new seeds that might be full of something different. If I am full of Him, full of love, obedience, purpose, and beauty He will blow me somewhere I can thrive and be seen.

As I wait on God, I am confident that He is moving me somewhere special. I have allowed Him to fill me and change me so that I can bear a fruit that pleases Him. In the waiting He is there. He speaks to me. He reminds me how precious I am to Him, how much He loves me, and that He has purpose for my life which He is carrying me toward.

I may be a dandelion seed blowing in the wind. I know

that God tells the wind where to carry me. My strength is in Him. So I may fly, but it is only because He is carrying me. I am thankful He blows me in the direction He chooses. He sees where all paths lead and knows the places He has made for me. In this way He carries me from glory to glory.

17:GOEL

Redeemer

He is near that justifieth me:
Who will contend with me?
Let us stand together:
Who is mine adversary?
Let him come near to me.
Isaiah 50:8 KJV

There is a readiness in me to fight. I've been like a boxer in the ring bouncing up and down, eager to fight, ready to move. The desire to do good and fight for light and truth is built into me. I would never want to miss an opportunity to deliver a blow to darkness, and to hear heaven cheer me on. Everyday, I step into the ring ready to fight. The difficult part is the fight is inside of me. My enemy is inside of me, so much so that it is me. The loudest voice in my head is my own. It is the hardest to silence when all I want to do is listen to what God has to tell me.

This is an impossible fight. There is no way I could look within myself and weed out what is wrong. This fight doesn't look like a fight. It looks more like death. In fact fighting here is more like giving up. More like laying down and allowing God to cut out pieces of me. There are things that have grown in me because of the world I live in. When I say grown in me, it is more like grown with me. The hurts that happened as a child, the desires that were placed in my heart by the world as I grew, and plenty of more hurts along the way they all became a part of me. God offered to remove those things. He doesn't just take them though, I have to look at what He shows me and then offer it up to Him. I could never find it all on my own. I wouldn't know how to get rid of it if I did.

This is why Jesus came to earth and took on sin and death. There is no way I can wrap my head around all that was accomplished with His life and death. I am too limited by my physical self. What I can see brings me to my knees everytime. There is nothing I would not lay at the foot of the cross. Nothing. So that is exactly what I do. Every piece of me, every want, every need, everything one at a time gets laid at the foot of the cross. Until every part of me has died with Him.

I can not fully understand what Jesus did while His physical body lay in that tomb for three days. I can not understand the magnitude of His victory. I only know what His word says and what He chooses to reveal to me. I know the victory is His, and because I am His the victory is mine too. I know that death does not hold me. The same resurrection power that rose Jesus from the grave lives in me.

18:YAHWEH-TSIDKENU

The Lord Our Righteousness

"And I say unto you, Ask, and it shall be given you; seek, and ye shall find; knock, and it shall be opened to you. For everyone that asketh receiveth; and he that seeketh findeth; and to him that knocketh it shall be opened. If a son shall ask bread of any of you that is a father, will he give him a stone? Or if he ask a fish, will he for a fish give him a serpent? Or if he shall ask an egg, will he offer him a scorpion? If ye then being evil, know how to give good gifts unto your children how much more shall your heavenly Father give the Holy Spirit to them that ask Him?"
Luke 11:9-13 KJV

I do not know where I am going. I know God has shown me things He wants to give me. I don't know how it will all come to pass, or when. I am dependent on Him completely. Trusting that not only will He lead me to where I need to be, but that He will take care of me along the way. This is trickier because I have three daughters who depend on me. So I am not only trusting Him with myself, but trusting Him with them as well. He has promised to not let me be ashamed or confounded. He has promised to meet my every need and I trust in His goodness and mercy. Because I am a mother I know a deeper love. I can see that I would never take things away from my children unless it was for their own good. I want them to be happy and fulfilled and thriving. I trust that He loves me even more than I love them.

My children have no choice but to trust me. I am all they have ever known. They were delivered out of me and into my arms whether they liked it or not. There is nothing quite like the feeling of becoming a mother. I felt my life had meaning for the first time. It gave me a sense of purpose I didn't know I could have. I was the only mother this person would ever have. The responsibility felt crushing at first. Where did I run? To my mother. She assured me that I was qualified to handle it. She happily let me stay with her for a few days after Sophia was born, to help me get my bearings. I learned how to be a mother from having a mother first, and then from becoming a mother. It was definitely a process, one I am still working on and I expect I will be for the rest of my life in one way or another.

God is my Father, but it is different. He is a Father who chose me. He wasn't just surprised at my birth, not sure what He was getting. He formed me to be exactly who I am, every piece. He placed me in the time and place and family He wanted me in. He knew exactly where I would go and what I would do every moment of every day before He made me. I can not surprise him. He loved me before He made me, knowing everything even then. As someone subject to time, that is a hard pill to swallow. There is nothing I have done, can do, or will do that can separate His love from me. He loves me and that is an unchangeable fact. Why is it so hard for me to believe the wonderful things He tells me,to believe I am worthy of that kind of love? Because, I am not worthy. It doesn't matter. It's mine because He says it is. I have learned that faith in God means sometimes I don't argue just because I can't comprehend. If God says it is so, it is so.

19:MAGEN

Shield

Praise Ye the Lord, O give thanks unto the Lord; for
he is good; for his mercy endureth forever.
Psalm 106:1 KJV

I was having a rough day. It was what felt like day 7,986 of the fire. I am sure I am overly dramatic, and can almost feel Jesus rolling his eyes. He took the heat but I was still there and it was stressful. Anyway, I was having a day. Just feeling cranky and like I was hanging by a thread. I was walking out to get the mail. As I walked to the mailbox I was talking to God. I said "Come one this day is getting me, Can I get something good in the mail? Just a little something to make me feel better." I don't know what I was expecting, but just a little bright spot in the day. I have a tiny glimmer of hope as I open the mailbox. There is one envelope in it. I pull it out. On the front of the envelope written in very large print is "It's a good day for things to go wrong!" Honestly, it takes my breath away. The first belly laugh is out of shock, come on this is the opposite of what I asked for. First point, the opposite of what I ask for is exactly what I need usually, and then again in some way turns out to be exactly what I asked for. I laughed all the way back from the mailbox. The envelope was an ad for extra insurance for the things in your home. The point of the ad was that even if things go wrong, it's good because you are covered and you have their insurance. Could this be any more perfect? I asked for just a little pick me up in the mailbox expecting money or something, and God as always goes way above and beyond.

This envelope has given me more encouragement than any check could have. He was reminding me, it doesn't matter how things look, it doesn't matter what might go wrong. I am covered. I know with God anything bad that happens he will flip and turn into something so good, that I won't even remember it seemed bad at first.

Another word He gave me the other day showed me a Pendulum. God is my restorative force. When evil pushes and swings my life into what looks like misfortune, God pulls me not only back to center but way over into his goodness. He is more constant than gravity, I can rest assured that as dark as things might look for a moment they will soon get equally bright. Oh how I love seeing his light illuminate the dark. There is nothing like it.

20:EL ELYON

God Most High

Remember ye not the former things, neither consider the things of old. Behold, I will do a new thing now it shall spring forth; shall ye not know it? I will even make a way in the wilderness, and rivers in the desert. Isaiah 43:18-19 KJV

Everything has mass. When I say everything I mean everything. Not just the physical things, my emotions, my thoughts, my desires, my sadness, my prayers, I mean everything. Mass and gravity are linked, so are mass and time. There is a balance that has to be kept within me. One that I do not understand how to measure. God does. When I come to him with a request I know there will be work he needs to do before I can receive what I have asked. If what I am asking to receive is something with great mass, I will need to be trained so I can carry that weight. Just like lifting heavy weights in the gym. He has me pick up the desire, to hold it in my mind and heart so that it is real to me, it feels like mine. Then he has me lay it back down.

This may not seem like much but God has a way of making things real. It might be real at this point I am not sure. He has let me hold a life in my heart and in my mind. He gives me confirmation that it is real throughout the day. He lets me see what I desire for my life becoming real so much that I feel like I have already lived it in some way. In the waiting for it all to come to pass the weight of what I want crushes me. It makes it impossible to breathe, to appreciate what is happening in the moment. The very fact that I am in constant communion with my creator should be and is enough, but all I could see was the future I wanted. So He says, lay it back down, give it back to me. I do not know how to lay it down fully. I tell Him I want to lay it down for Him but I don't know how on my own. He helps me to give it back. It felt like I died, again.

He lets me rest. My mind is restored, and my spirit. I am able to enjoy Him again. I even start to see the beauty in each day. I am enjoying my life again, not just living through the waiting. I know that if He said yes, it is as good as done. He is helping me get strong enough to hold the massive weight of the life I desire. Then He asks me to take the desire again. I do. This time I think I must not be holding it. I can't even feel it. Barely think about it at all. He assures me I am holding it, I am just stronger, and it is in the right place now, beneath Him.

21:SHAPHAT
Judge

But now, God's message, The God who made you in the first place, Jacob, the One who got you started, Israel: Don't be afraid, I've redeemed you. I've called your name. You're mine. When you're in over your head, I'll be there with you. When you're in rough waters, you will not go down. When you're between a rock and a hard place, it won't be a dead end- because I am God, your personal God, The Holy of Israel, your Savior. I paid a huge price for you: All of Egypt, with rich Cush and Seba thrown in! That's how much you mean to me! That's how much I love you! I'd sell off the whole world to get you back, trade the creation just for you! So don't be afraid: I'm with you.

I'll round up all your scattered children, pull them in from east and west. I'll send orders north and south: 'Send them back. Return my sons from distant lands, my daughters from faraway places. I want them back, every last one who bears my name, every man, woman, and child. Whom I created for my glory, yes, personally formed and made each one.'

Get the blind and deaf out here and ready- the blind (though there's nothing wrong with their eyes) and the deaf (though there's nothing wrong with their ears. Then get the other nations out here and ready. Let's see what they have to say about this, how they account for what's happened. Let them present their expert witnesses, and make their case; Let them try to convince us what they say is true.

"But you are my witnesses." God's Decree. "You're my handpicked servant, so that you'll come to know and trust me, understand both that I am, and who I am. Previous to me there was no such thing as a god, nor will there be after me. I, yes I, am God. I'm the only Savior there is. I spoke, I saved, I told you what existed long before these upstart gods appeared on the scene.

And you know it, you're my witnesses,
you're the evidence." God's Decree.
"Yes, I am God. I've always been God and I always will be God.
No one can take anything from me. I make; who can unmake it?"
Isaiah 43:1-13 MSG

God's truth is too good to not believe. He made me in such a way, that He must be my everything, in doing so He makes me in His image, like Him. He gives me an honor even the angels could envy. When I open my eyes to Him, to His wonder, He fills me and makes me into what I was created to be. He tells me He loves me in every way I can imagine and so many more. There is no good thing He would withhold from me, and all good things are found in Him. When I turn my face fully to Jesus, I find everything I ever wanted, and more than I knew I could want.

When He speaks to me, He speaks wonderful things over me. He also brought it to my attention that I have a very hard time hearing the really good stuff. I am quick to jump to any conclusion that seems like things are going to get difficult, or I have work to be done. When He tells me I am perfect and He loves me and has the most incredible things in store for me, I have to remind myself that if He says it, it is true. I know I don't deserve His love. Part of the dying process is killing the part of me that is unwilling to accept the forgiveness Jesus has given me. I do not have the power to forgive myself. It is not my job. I do however have the power to counter any thought that says I'm guilty with a stamp that says paid in full. There is nothing the cross doesn't cover. So while I can't wrap my head around the forgiveness it takes to let go of what I've done, I can refuse to accept the thoughts that creep into my mind declaring me guilty or that say I have a price to pay. He paid it all. The best thing I can do is claim the gift He paid such a high price to give me. My thoughts are a battleground, the cross is the victory.

In the meantime, God has made me not just a daughter, but a witness. I am a witness to his mercy and goodness. In order to be a witness, I must first witness it. He says that I am His handpicked servant. In order to know and trust him, I must first know that He is, and who He is. It all starts with being able to accept the fact that He is. Once I accepted that He is, how could I not want to seek him and know him? In seeking him, I found him. He was happy to show me who He is. He even wrote a whole book to let everyone know. The book is not really worth reading though if I don't believe that He is. He doesn't stop with the Bible. He speaks, He moves, He works in me in undeniable ways. He is turning my life into the evidence of who He is, what greater honor or blessing could I ever ask for?

22:TO TRUST
IS TO PRAY

*For the Lord God will help me; Therefore shall I
not be confounded: Therefore have I set my face like a
flint, and I know that I shall not be ashamed.*
Isaiah 50:7 KJV

God is not pushy. If I ever feel like I'm being nagged by a pushy salesman, I can rest assured that is not from God. His voice is an instruction sometimes, but in that instruction there is clarity. He doesn't say well if you want..... Then you should probably... He tells me my next move and I make it. Sometimes the move makes sense to me, although usually it is not in the way I thought at the time. Usually, it doesn't make sense at the time. He sees pieces on the board I can not. I know this.

When I don't know the next way to move, I stop. I trust Him with it by giving my next move to Him in prayer. Once I have given it to Him, my mind is clear. It is not my thought to hold anymore. I don't try and figure it out because I can not. He does. My mind is not working on it, so when the answer comes I know it was from Him not from me. I can be confident in what He says to do.

23:MY REST COMES WHEN I LET GOD FIGHT FOR ME.

And Moses said unto the people, Fear ye not, stand still, and see the salvation of the Lord, which He will shew to you today: For the Egyptians whom you have seen today, you shall see them again no more for ever. The Lord shall fight for you, and ye shall hold your peace.
Exodus 14:13-14 KJV

I have been given a life in God. I spend every moment I can fully aware that He is with me. The only time it gets difficult to keep Him at the front of my mind is when I am with other people. There is one way I have found to do this. To include Him in the conversation. This is where I get very obnoxious, very quickly to people who aren't ready to hear. He is me though, and I am in Him. If someone wants to be with me, then they will also have to be with Him. We are a pair. We don't go anywhere separate, I would rather not go, then leave Him out.

It isn't that I want to push Jesus down everyone's throat, I don't. That isn't the way people come to Jesus. So I have discovered the best thing I can do a lot of the time is sit and listen. That does not come easily for me. I like to entertain, and tell stories, and get laughs. God likes my stories and the laughs and all that too, but He is now in all my stories. So when I tell my story, He is part of it. This is good. If I dominate the conversation though, it feels like I am ramming Him down everyone's throat. This is why I am learning to listen more than I speak.

I am learning to actually hear what other people are trying to tell me, rather than wait for my turn to be in the spotlight. God has also shown me that when I listen to people, I am actually able to respond in the way they need. I can truly hear what they are saying and He can help me speak in a way that they can hear. Most people don't listen anymore; their minds are not conditioned to focus for longer than about thirty seconds before they are looking for what they will say next. So if I can actually listen to people, they might have a chance to voice what is really going on in their heads and feel heard by someone. Not only that but if I listen long enough to hear what is in their heart, God can give me the words they need to hear.

I can listen to Him when I am with other people because I have learned to listen to Him when I am alone. The loudest voice has always been my own. Once I learned to be silent and listen to His voice instead of my own. I realized the anxieties and troubles I had been facing were a result of what I had been speaking over myself. I had constantly been assuring myself that the next bill wouldn't get paid, unless... or I would never be happy, unless... or there would be a problem with the kids, or the car, or the house, unless.... The "... " was always the part my mind was scrambling to solve. How to fix an enormous list of problems that never even existed. Now I am silent, I do not accept problems I don't see. If a problem arises I don't even see it as a problem anymore. I see it as an opportunity.

It is a good day for things to go wrong. Why? Because I am covered. God loves an opportunity to refill me, to show me He is there. When do I appreciate a miracle the most? When I need it the most. God is never late, and always on time. He teaches me to trust in the waiting. What He does is perfect. It often feels like free falling, but He is with me holding my hand telling me He's got me. He fights for me, all I have to do is keep my peace, and when I can't keep mine, He gives me His. The problems I faced I assure you they are gone and I will never see them again.

24:ABHIR

Mighty One

Lead me in thy truth, and teach me;
For Thou art the God of my salvation;
On Thee do I wait all the day.
Psalm 25:5 KJV

There is a mass involved in the decisions I make every day. Different decisions, different weights. When I add up the weight of every little decision I make every day it is substantial. I offer up every decision to God. My life is a sacrifice, an act of worship. I wouldn't want it any other way. When I give Him all those moments, all those choices, what He gives me in return is so much more. He gives me confidence in every step. When I move in His will. I am unstoppable. Every single step I take is the right one. Even if I misunderstand and step wrong, He makes it right.

I heard someone once say "God loves it when we step out in faith, even if we are mistaken in what He has asked us to do." This changed my life. God sees the intent of my heart. If I am seeking His will with my whole heart and trying to act in it. He will bless me. Even if I fall down over and over again, He will continue to pick me up and eventually I will be running. I just need the confidence to take the first steps in faith. So if I am seeking God and I take steps in faith believing it is what He wants I can't go wrong. He loves it. It brings Him joy. If I keep my eyes on Him, eventually my stumbling, fumbling walk becomes a run.

When all of my mass is centered in God, my life begins to spin around Him and He pulls me in closer like a leaf in a whirlpool. I give him my thoughts, my actions, my everything. The gravity of my life is nothing compared to His gravity. Surrendering my nothing for His everything I am drawn into His power, His care, His purpose. My life becomes a part of His mighty river and I am flooded with all the goodness that He carries.

25:KANNA

Jealous, Zealous

Examine me, O Lord, and prove me; try my reins and my heart.
Psalm 26:2 KJV

"I don't know where I'm going, but I know that I'm chasing after you." That's the first line in one of my favorite songs. I feel that, and it's good to know that I'm not the only one feeling that. Even though sometimes it's hard to believe that such a deeply personal experience is something that is shared with so many others. God says I am the apple of His eye, His daughter. Jesus tells me He did it all for me, and He would do it all again even if I were the only one He was saving. There is a closeness and a love between He and I that I don't want to share with anyone else, and at the same time I want everyone else to be able to experience what I am experiencing.

There is a level of intimacy and connection that I could never have with any other person. No one could ever know me like He does. He knows me better than I know myself, and He loves me more than anyone. It takes walking with Him and talking with Him daily to be able to begin to comprehend what that means. In conversation I have asked Him to explain how He can love me like He does and walk and talk with me like He does, and still do the same with everyone else. This is something I don't think I can actually understand yet. He explained that the best way I can think about it is that He is really big, bigger than I can fathom. So big it is best if I think of it like I have my own personal Jesus. One that exists just for me. I don't have to be jealous or worried because He is all mine devoted to me. He is so big and so great that everyone has their own personal Jesus. I have a Jesus who knows me inside and out. He has paid for my sins on the cross and would do it again just for me. This would probably be an explanation similar to how you would explain theoretical physics to a two year old, very very simplified. It helps me though.

I don't need to ever be worried about His affection or attention. He is always there just for me. I don't ever have to think of sharing Jesus like I am giving up a piece of something to someone else. I am not. I am only helping Jesus reach another piece of Himself that He is longing to have. The more people I bring to Jesus the more rich and full the whole is made. My piece rejoices when other pieces are brought in. It only makes me stronger and more fulfilled.

God tells me right from the beginning He is a jealous God. In no uncertain terms He lays it right out. Do not put anything before Him. He is jealous. Jealousy doesn't seem like a good attribute to have, but neither does anger and God has both. If he possesses them there must be some way in which they are good. I think anger is an easier one to justify. Anger in the face of evil is easy to justify. Jealousy however might need a little help.

There is a love or possessiveness attributed to jealousy. I would not want someone who is irrational and prone to violence jealous for me. However, if I had a husband whom I loved and trusted and I knew to be reasonable and loved me dealy, I would feel like he didn't love me if he didn't feel some jealousy over me. Because God is perfect, always justified, always right, He is the embodiment of love, His jealousy is just another way I know how deep His love for me is.

He cares deeply where I put my heart, where I spend my time, and where my focus lies. Not only does He long for me to be with Him, He knows that nothing else can fill the place in my life that He was meant to fill. If I put anything above Him it will end up hurting me. He doesn't want me hurt. If I try to live my life without Him, I will not only be missing out on the entire purpose of life, I will end up crushed by what I try to replace Him with. When I put Him first, He orders everything else in my life and in my heart.

26:EYALUTH

Strength

The Lord is my light and my salvation; Whom shall I fear?
The Lord is the strength of my life; of whom shall I be afraid?
Psalm 27:1 KJV

It is a strange thing to have my entire world change, but yet nothing outside of me has changed. The way I interact with things have changed, which changes things some. My relationships are all much better. My house is cleaner, my yard looks nicer, and I am a better steward of my time. My circumstances have not changed yet, but the way I move in life has completely changed. I know there is a point where my life will catch up with me, I just don't know when that is. God has told me that I asked for alot of things all at once, and that is exactly what He is doing. Waiting to give them to me all at once. He likes to go big. When He moves He wants us all to know it was Him.

All of my faith and all of my energy go into the things unseen. This is exhausting for more reasons than I realize. Like that dolphin living with its head above the water most of the time, it gets tiring. God didn't just stop at teaching me how to swim like a dolphin coming up for air. He's teaching me to jump out of the air and do tricks too. I wanted it all, He is giving it all. I am so grateful, and so tired. I wouldn't trade it for anything though. He might be keeping me in a safe harbor at the moment and teaching me, but I know I won't be here forever. He is preparing me to swim out into open waters.

Where He leads me I will follow. I don't know the dangers

of the places He is preparing me to go. I do know that I can trust Him to lead me and to make me strong enough to handle whatever I may face. There is no depth too deep for Him to come find me and rescue me.

27:TSADDIQ

Righteous One

Many are the afflictions of the righteous:
But the Lord delivereth him out of them all.
Psalm 34:19 KJV

Righteous means morally right, justifiable, virtuous. If I look inside at why I do the things I do, there is almost always a root of selfishness. Something I will gain from my action, even if it is just a morally superior feeling, or the knowledge that God is watching and approves. Rarely are my actions ever purely righteous, if they are I would say that it must be the Holy Spirit acting on my behalf. I know me, God knows me. He calls me righteous anyway.

One morning I woke up, the day before had been a struggle. I had made it through but it took a toll on me. The next morning I woke up to a song playing in my head. Loudly, unmistakably not from me. As soon as I opened my eyes it was like someone pushed play. "I see you dressed in white, every wrong made right, I see a rose in bloom at the sight of you, oh so priceless." It continued. I got up and popped in my airpods and felt the Holy Spirit moving in me. It was like God Himself was singing the song to me telling me how He sees me and how much He loves me. I had really been struggling and worried about what needed to be fixed in me next. Seeing the problems instead of what He sees. He sees it as done. He sees me whole and perfect and blooming like I was always meant to. I am dressed in white, irreplaceable, and priceless to Him. God sees me as righteous already. I need to start seeing myself that way. He promises to deliver me from all of my afflictions. I just have to let Him.

28:EL-OLAM

Everlasting God

Let the words of my mouth, and the meditation
of my heart, be acceptable in thy sight,
O Lord, my strength, and my redeemer.
Psalm 19:14 KJV

God's love and blessings are always flowing, always. He never stops. He never gets tired, he never changes. He is the same yesterday, today, and forever. I am always changing, always growing. It is when I stop changing that I get concerned. I am meant to grow here on earth. That is why the most uncomfortable and frightening place to be is the place where I am stagnant. When I spend time with Him He leads me so that I am not still and stuck. When my heart is in Him, He continually whispers to it so that it feels new each day.

There is continual growth in God. No matter how far I go I know He can always take me farther. The promised land for me is eternity, with Him. I will be happy to wander through this desert the rest of my life as long as He is with me. With God even the desert feels like a blessing. It is a place of continual learning. I know there will be different seasons in my life, but that just assures change as well.

Not only will I change, but my relationship with God is always growing and changing. As He calls me to do different things, sometimes that requires that He speak to me in different ways. In order to fulfill the purposes He has for me I have to be willing to trust that whatever new thing He requires of me, He will make me able to do. God tends to give tasks that are impossible. It always makes me smile when He gives me a job I can not do. The harder the job the better. Because I know the harder it is the closer I will need to be to Him to accomplish it.

When I think about the fact that He doesn't need me to do anything. He is perfectly capable of doing anything He wants apart from me. He gives me these things, for me. Because I get so excited about the things He asks me to do. He has shown me things He is going to give me to do in the future. Things that right now make me chuckle because it seems so impossible. Good. The more impossible, the better. If I need him leading me through every step and every breath in order to accomplish it, then I know that is exactly where He will be.

In contemplating Him, and what He wants for my life I am drawn closer. This is what pleases Him. God loves it when I think about my life and where it will go, as long as I include Him. If I leave Him out, what should be looking forward with eager anticipation and wonder, turns to anxiety. When I know Him and trust Him fully I know He is taking care of me. I don't have to know where I am going, how I will get there, or even how long it will take. It has never been about getting there. I am here on this earth to walk with the King of the Universe, The Maker of Heaven and Earth, The Great I am. There is nothing and no one higher than Him, and He wants nothing more than to be with me. Why would I ever be in a hurry to go anywhere, when I am with Him?

29:ZUR

God Our Rock

*The Lord will perfect that which concerneth me: Thy mercy O
Lord, endureth forever: forsake not the works of thine own hands.
Psalm 138:8 KJV*

My trouble doesn't usually lie in trusting God, the trust
issues I have are with myself. God has begun showing me that
trusting myself and trusting Him go hand in hand. This is one
of the excuses I use frequently, and get called out on when I am
worrying. "Well God I trust you, it's me I don't trust, what if I
heard you wrong, or what if I'm crazy, or greedy, or just bad and
I don't realize that I'm going down a wrong way because I got
tricked by the devil" and it can go on and on.

Sometimes God uses a little snippet from a movie to get
a point across. It will play in my head. When I get in a place of
arguing with myself or circular logic and I start to make myself
crazy. He shows me the little guy from the princess bride trying
to deduce which cup has the poison in it. I laugh and remember
he never asked me to figure things out. He said He would show
me. In fact He clearly tells me quite often, "quit trying to figure
it out, you can't. The more you try the further away from the
answer you get. I will show you if you stop trying to do it
yourself."

Now I am not saying God doesn't want me to use my brain,
He does. He just needs me to be quiet and listen sometimes
though. When there are pieces in play I can't even see, it is not
something I can figure out on my own. He is loving enough to
tell me when to think about something and when to just listen

and watch Him work.

When I say that I trust Him, but I don't trust myself, He reminds me that He never asked me to trust myself. He asked me to trust Him completely. In trusting Him completely I also trust that He can even protect me from myself. I already know the biggest enemy I face is inside of me, He is also well aware of that fact. He's the one who pointed it out. So if I trust Him. I trust that He will not let the devil lead me to destruction. He will not let me wander off confused. If I leave the path and His plan, it will be because I did it knowingly and willfully. Here is where he puts the snippet of Ben Stiller saying "I know you, you know you, you know that I know that you know I know you." This makes me laugh because of course I choose Him. I have nothing to worry about. He has me. The only thing I have to trust myself with is to choose Him. God and I both know beyond the shadow of a doubt that I will always choose Him.

30:LONGING

He is my destination

The Lord is gracious, and full of compassion;
slow to anger, and of great mercy.
The Lord is good to all: and his tender mercies are over all his works.
Psalm 145:8-9 KJV

Patience is defined as the capacity to tolerate delay, trouble, or suffering without getting angry or upset. I can say that God has been working on my patience in miraculous ways lately. A few months ago I would get upset at every stop light because drivers can't sit through a red light without looking at their phone, and then inevitably the light turns green, and we are all still sitting behind someone who forgot they were in a car because the phone came out. See I just had a little flare up thinking about it, but I'm ok now. Learning patience means learning to tolerate delay, trouble, and suffering.

I think the first step was learning to tolerate it, it took awhile before I stopped getting angry or upset. What changed things for me is reminding myself Who is with me. When I know that God Himself is in the car at the stoplight with me, and presumably with the person on their phone as well, it changes things. First of all, if He is with me then I am where I need to be. Yes, sometimes I still have to be somewhere at a certain time. When I slow down during my day though and let him help me order my steps, I am usually running on time and a slow driver can't make me late. There are instances though where something happens and I am late. Even if it was my fault, there is only so much I can do. I do not like to be late. It frustrates me but if for some reason I am late, then maybe I am supposed to be late, maybe not. God reminds me it's a good day for things to go wrong. I am covered. I won't let it bother me. That is just the delay part of the picture.

Trouble can look alot like delay. A stumbling block in the path of where I want to be. Until I remember who is with me, and that as long as I am with Him I am where I need to be. Still when something happens to my car, I fall through my deck, the dishwasher breaks, or any other number of things I remember Who is with me. There is nothing He can not do. No problem He can not solve. If I slow down and listen to Him, He will help me. Just like that, trouble turns into opportunity. It is an opportunity to listen, to learn, and to watch Him work.

Suffering should be harder for me but somehow I am most patient in suffering. I have seen suffering. I know loss. I think it has always been in suffering when patience was not as hard. In suffering is when I always found myself wrapped firmly in His arms. There was never a need to move when I found myself in suffering. He has always held me close and whispered that we will sit through it together. Sitting wrapped in the arms of my maker I don't need patience.

The key to patience anyway I look at it is remembering I am exactly where I need to be as long as I have Him. The more closely I follow Him, the more confident I can be that I am exactly where I should be. He is never late. There is no trouble he can't fix. Suffering can not compare to the warmth of His embrace.

31: WORSHIP

I lay my life on the altar.

But the hour cometh, and now is, when the true
worshippers shall worship the Father in spirit and in truth:
for the Father seeketh such to worship Him.
God is a spirit: and they that worship Him
must worship Him in spirit, and in truth.
John 4:23-24 KJV

God is constant, His creation all bows to Him. People are the wildcard. We have a choice. Everything about a wildcard is up to the discretion of the player. Therein lies the trouble. I am playing a game I do not understand. I do not know the rules, I cannot see all of the board, and I have no idea what I am capable of.

When my kids were little and we would play games, if one of them was having trouble or not doing well, they would get a bright idea. They would decide we were playing on teams, and they wanted to be on my team. They would throw all their cards or monopoly money or whatever over with me and now what I had was theirs and what they had was mine. I have carried all of my pieces, cards, monopoly money, whatever and thrown it into God's lap. I want to be on His team. He happily accepted my offer. He will even let me make the moves if I want to, and He won't be mad about it. He is also very happy to give me instruction so that I can become a better player. He wants me to win, and to have fun doing it. The more I let him help me the better I do.

There are other players in the game too. Some are playing on their own, some are on God's team like me, and then some are on the team of the enemy. The enemy is not like God. He has already lost the game. Like a spoiled child who doesn't accept defeat, he wanders around manipulating people. He gets them to make the same bad moves he made. Maybe it's because misery loves company, maybe he is just trying to take players away from God's team, or maybe it's something deeper and darker than I care to understand right now. God sees all the players. He knows who He is helping. He knows who is trying to do it on their own. He also knows who is being led by the enemy.

The enemy is a master manipulator, and a great deceiver. The people who he leads are just like him. They can manipulate and deceive with ease. So much so that it might be impossible to recognize them for who and what they are without the Holy Spirit leading me. There are no rules for them, they can preach in a church just as easily as they can sell children on the street. They know who they are serving, I might not. God wants me to love everyone, and that means every single person. He doesn't want me to let everyone into my life, or into the lives of my children. I can feel love and compassion for a person who has been so deeply deceived by the father of lies that they now follow him openly and knowingly. I will not allow them access to my life or my children though. There are people that God must deal with. He may use me sometimes to show love, or share truth with anyone. He has also made it abundantly clear that I am not to bring people into my life without speaking to Him first.

When God began moving in my life and using me in the way I asked Him to, He separated me from everyone. It is just He and I. He has slowly started adding some people back. People are the wildcard though. I need Him to tell me who and what to let into my life. I can show love and kindness to everyone I meet without fully making them a part of my life. When the enemy sees me winning in the game, He will want to take me out of the game. He can't do it himself. God won't let him. That leaves him two options. He can manipulate me into destroying myself. I am covered by the blood of Jesus, I am filled with the Holy Spirit, I spend all day long with God in prayer, and I have the word of God written on my heart. He can't get me that way. That leaves him only one other option. He will send his best players to try and infiltrate my life. Master manipulators and deceivers who are seeking to hurt me in any way they can. God wants to make sure I don't let my guard down and open the door to a wolf dressed in sheep's clothing.

I don't have to worry about it. God thinks of everything. He makes sure I know where the danger lies. He tells me the next step before I take it. I only have to remember not to get excited and sprint off ahead. When it looks like I am winning I have to remember why I am winning.

32:KADOSH

Holy One

The Lord is my Shepherd; I shall not want.
He maketh me to lie down in green pastures:
He leadeth me beside the still waters.
He restoreth my soul: He leadeth me in the
paths of righteousness for His name's sake.
Yea, though I walk through the valley of the
shadow of death, I will fear no evil:
For thou art with me; thy rod and thy staff they comfort me.
Thou preparest a table before me in the presence of mine enemies:
Thou anointest my head with oil; my cup runneth over.
Surely goodness and mercy shall follow me all the days of my life:
And I will dwell in the house of the Lord forever.
Psalm:23 KJV

I have learned to go slowly. One of my favorite songs "The Slower I go", says "Teach me and know me and prune what you find, the future I made Oh I leave it behind, If it's you Lord it's perfect in timing. I wanna go slowly, this moment is holy, you're never in a hurry. So why ever would I be? It seems as though the slower I go the faster I arrive." There was a week or so where I had to sing that song to myself many many times a day. My tendency is to rush. When I get excited, I am rushing to get more, or to make it to whatever I am excited about. When I get bored I am in a rush to get to the next thing. When I get tired, I rush to the time when I can rest. The list goes on and on and on.

When I see each single moment as Holy as perfect, I am in no rush. If God wanted me in another moment or another place that is where I would be. Trusting him is trusting in his absolute authority and power. Even if I have gotten myself into a pickle. The only reason He hasn't yoinked me right out, is because there is something to be gained in the waiting. There is growth in pain, refining in fire, and faith built in waiting. These are only the benefits that I can see and feel with my own eyes. I know that God is bigger than anything I can see and so is his goodness.

When I sit in the moment calmly, with Him. I have peace. When I have peace, my mind is quiet. When my mind is quiet, I hear Him so clearly. When I hear Him, I learn, I grow, I change, and that moves me. So the slower that I go, the faster I arrive.

Everytime I think I have found the greatest level of trust I can have, He takes me deeper. There is even more to trust Him with. There is nothing He can not do. In the stillness, in the quiet, in the slow times, this is when I am actually moving the fastest. When I stop running, and let Him hold me, and talk with me, I realize He has been carrying me to places I could've never ran on my own.

33:LET MY HEART BE A REFLECTION OF GOD'S HEART

Fear not; for thou shalt not be ashamed; neither be thou confounded: for thou shalt not be put to shame; for thou shalt forget the shame of thy youth, and shalt not remember the reproach of thy widowhood anymore. For thy maker, is thine husband, the Lord of Hosts is his name; and thy redeemer The Holy One of Israel; The God of the whole earth shall he be called.
Isaiah 54:4-5 KJV

There is a beauty that exists when God works through people. He creates harmony and love and joy. When one person is able to step in and fill a need because they listened to Him, another person's prayer is answered and their faith made stronger. We need Him. Being around other people who live in Him strengthens us in ways being alone cannot. He is all I need. Being with Him fulfills me. He is a loving Father and wants even more for me. He wants me to have friends. I let Him be my best friend first and He shows me what real friendship looks like. He wants to give me everything, including the blessing and strength that comes with being surrounded by other believers.

He also wants me to minister to unbelievers, to spread His word and His love to everyone. When I am strong in Him, and strengthened with the fellowship of other believers, I can walk freely anywhere ministering to anyone without fear. God put in my heart a need to be around other people as well as Him. If I walk into the world without having that need met in a healthy way, I am susceptible to the enemy's attack. It is easier to infiltrate my life with people who intend to do me harm. When I let him fill my life with brothers and sisters in Christ, I can confidently walk into the world ministering to anyone and everyone knowing I won't be tempted for companionship in someone God has not sent me.

There is a way to love people and show them Christ, and still know that they are not meant to be joined to my life. There is a level of trust and confidence that comes with knowing God has sent them into my life. There is a quote I love by Maya Angelou, "A woman's heart should be so hidden in God that a man has to seek Him just to find her." I shouldn't look for a husband, I should look to God. He will give me the desires of my heart. I shouldn't go searching for best friends, mentors, confidants. I should keep seeking Him and He will make my life full and make me whole.

I've heard it said an open mind is an empty mind. That might be true. If I leave my mind open to hearing God's voice, I have to let my own thoughts go. What I have noticed though is that what God speaks doesn't leave my mind, even when the doors are open. His word, the truths He speaks to me take root in my mind. The lies of the enemy, the scenarios I create in my head flow in and out like the tide. The truths of God do not budge. The more I collect, the more I retain. I don't have to work to keep it in, it just stays.

When God first began pouring into me, it was like being blasted with a firehose of information sometimes, or a raging river rushing through my thoughts. I would barely catch a glimpse of one thing and realize it before the next was there. I had asked for an accelerated growth phase, and God delivered in ways I could've never imagined. As I always do, I found a way to worry. I told him I would never be able to remember everything. He kind of laughed and asked me if I thought He was able to tell me again. Then He started to bring to mind things I had forgotten, and the instant one flicker or part of the picture came to mind, it was like the whole experience returned. He has taken me through so many experiences quickly, and let me work my way through so many realizations one after another. There is no way to sit back and look at it all at once. Instead, He waits until the exact moment I need to remember something and then brings it to my memory. He said it is better that I feel like I have forgotten everything sometimes. When I need it He can pull it right out in a miraculous fashion and there will be no doubt it is from Him.

In this way I can go out into the world, and as I listen to people God sometimes brings a particular memory or realization or metaphor He showed me to light in my mind. I have already had time to process what it means so that I am not floundering to figure it out on the spot. I can be confident that I am supposed to share it with them because up until that very moment it had been lost in the recesses of my thoughts. I don't always know what to do, but in knowing that I don't know, I know. He has told me when I don't know what to do, just wait. We are never in a hurry, never have been, never will be. When I need to move He speaks and His orders come with clarity. I don't usually know the reason why I am doing something but I know what I need to do and I know that it is from Him.

34:EL GIBHOR

Mighty God

What doth the Lord God require of thee, but to fear the Lord thy God,
to walk in all His ways, and to love Him, and to serve the Lord thy God,
with all thy heart and with all thy soul, to keep the commandments of
the Lord, and his statutes, which I command thee this day for thy good?
Deuteronomy 10:12-13 KJV

Last night while I was laying in bed. Just talking to God while I get sleepy like I do every night. He asked if I wanted another word to think about, so He gave me the word, and I began saying it in my head and just sort of clearing my mind while I said it. After a while I could see a geyser. I didn't really understand but sat and thought about it. Ok, so a geyser has this pent up energy under the earth that has to be released and that is where it comes out, I think. "Keep going", He said. I started thinking about God, and how God is a God of miracles. He wants to part seas, move mountains, heal, do big things. If God just did that stuff all the time throughout the years, we wouldn't need faith to believe in Him, He would just be part of life. The miracles would even lose their grandeur and magnificence because just like lightning and thunder and rainbows and flowers they would be part of everyday life. So He holds back. He waits. He lets us go for generations some times while He holds back. He still moves everywhere all the time, but it is in a stifled manner. He doesn't let His power be fully seen. In this we have to develop a different level of faith and we grow and change in different ways throughout those generations.

The thing about this is, when God holds back the Devil kind of holds back for a while too. He is still out there sneaking about doing his thing, He just hides his work better. Satan's work is best accomplished when we stop believing that He exists, and that God exists. When I look around the world today, it is obvious Satan is no longer hiding. He is out of the shadows taking the stage shouting that He is here. The only reason He would do this is because He knows God is about to show us who He is again.

God's time of holding back is almost over. Like all of the energy pent up under the earth spewing out in a geyser, He is going to come out in a million different ways all over the earth. The actual geysers will be people, He will move in and on. That is how His glory will be seen pouring out over the earth. Not just preaching and wisdom, in miraculous healings, people being lifted out of the street and set with kings, miracles in more ways than I can imagine, but the point is they will undoubtedly be miracles. If He parted the sea, we wouldn't believe it was Him. We would watch the T.V. and say it was CGI or China or something. These miracles will be personal, they will be seen in people we know and love. I am already a miracle, I can't believe what He has been doing with me and I know He is just getting started. I am a geyser waiting for Him to spew out of me, and make my life the evidence of Him

He told me once a while back "the unseen will be seen". I didn't fully understand what that meant but I could see the implications, and I see a little more of it every day. It might be the most exciting thing I have ever heard. God is ready, and so am I.

35: I AM A DROP OF WATER IN GOD'S RIVER

Trust in the Lord with all thine heart; and
lean not unto thine own understanding.
In all thy ways acknowledge Him, and He shall direct thy paths.
Proverbs 3:5-6 KJV

I like to go ice skating. I go maybe once every six years, but I like it when I do. When I do go, my confidence on skates is about .05 out of 10. This is to be expected because it has been six years since I've been skating. I start out on the edge of the rink wobbling and holding on as I go. Pretty soon I'm skating next to the wall without touching it but still close enough that if I need to reach out it's there. Eventually I am actually out on the rink skating in circles. One skating session is never enough to be confident out there, but I do make it out. Slightly wobbly and in a sort of constant state of anxiety, I would not be prepared for anything unexpected. God reminds me of this scenario when my mind tries to rush His process. When I feel stuck I have to remember God is just giving me some more laps around the rink to build my confidence. He's right here skating along with me giving me pointers.

It's funny how excitement and exhaustion are two polar opposites that can do the same thing. They overlap somehow. They both cloud my judgment. They both make me impulsive. They both are able to steal my joy and peace if I let them. There is a different kind of excitement that God has showed me. One that carries with it peace and joy for the moment. I can be excited about the promises of tomorrow and enjoy the moment right now. I have to recognize that right now is a piece of tomorrow. Part of my tomorrow is actually found in each moment.

There was a time when I kept taking the good things God would show me and then mark them on a calendar in my mind, making a sort of countdown. This always made me throw away the moment, it is impossible to enjoy now when your eyes are on tomorrow. One night as I was drifting off to sleep. I saw myself trying to hang a piece of bread up on the nail my calendar hangs on. It kept falling apart and it was frustrating me. Then it was over and I thought, um ok I don't really get it, but it was there in my brain. The next day as I was eating breakfast, I started daydreaming about my future and then wondering when and how much longer I have to wait. God clearly said "quit trying to take the bread I give you and hang it on the calendar." Instead of taking what He told me, the good things I have to look forward to and digesting it, then moving on. I was trying to put it on my calendar. Things are moving on His time, not mine. So now when He gives me a glimpse of something to look forward to, I think about it from time to time and it gives me joy for the future, but I don't put a delivery date on it.

36:LET MY HEART BEAT WITH YOURS

Happy is the man that findeth wisdom, and the man that getteth understanding. For the merchandise of it is better than the merchandise of silver, and the gain thereof than fine gold. She is more precious than rubies: and all the things thou canst desire are not to be compared unto her. Length of days is in her right hand; and in her left hand riches and honor. Her ways are of pleasantness, and all her paths are peace. She is a tree of life to them that lay hold upon her: and happy is every one that retaineth her.
Proverbs 3:13-18 KJV

I am a part of the body of Christ. The Holy Spirit is like the blood flowing through the body of Christ. It travels all over the body bringing life. It is the heart of Jesus that keeps it flowing through the body. The Holy Spirit brings me the spiritual oxygen I breathe. It strips away the impurities and carries them off to be purified. Without blood flowing through it no part of the body can live. Without the Holy Spirit I would be dead in Christ.

There are many people who have accepted the gift of salvation, but they never receive the Holy Spirit. The Holy Spirit is the only way I can be alive in Christ now. Without the Holy Spirit I am dead. God will not leave a piece of dead flesh connected to the bride he is preparing for Jesus. He wants the bride spotless and perfect. Not only is that dead flesh a blight, it would fester and begin to rot the flesh around it. If I want to remain in the body of Christ I must have the Holy Spirit. It is not optional.

How do I know if I have the Holy Spirit? I know because I feel the peace of Jesus over my life. I know because I have love in my heart that is not my own. I am able to look at the world with eyes like Jesus. When people treat me poorly, I see their pain. If I don't see this in the moment, it is the Holy Spirit that reminds me after. Having the Holy Spirit doesn't mean I am perfect. I am far from it. I have a teacher, a guide. When I am looking at something with human eyes, the Holy Spirit shows me a different way. The Holy Spirit is what teaches my heart to beat more like Jesus.

If I walk through life constantly bitter, and angry lashing out at people I am not operating in the Holy Spirit. If I walk through life always lusting after the next thing, never looking at God and what He wants, I am not operating in the Holy Spirit. It doesn't take much self examination to look at my life and thoughts and see if I am being guided and corrected, or if I am marching off in my own direction blindly.

When the members of the body of Christ are all filled with this life blood, they are all moving to the beat of Christ's heart as well. When we all move to the beat of His heart we are unstoppable. There is nothing we cannot accomplish for Him. This is where I want to be. Marching to the beat of His heart with my brothers and sisters and accomplishing His will. Being made spotless and perfect in preparation for that day when my longing is over, and I can finally stand face to face with the one I love.

37: I AM A WAVE ON THE OCEAN OF GOD'S LOVE

Withhold not good from them to whom it is due, when it is in the power of thine hand to do it.   Proverbs 3:27 KJV

Never walk away from someone who deserves help; your hand is God's hand for that person.   Proverbs 3:27 MSG

My whole life I have heard people describe their walk with Jesus. I have heard it in countless testimonies, poetry, books, and songs. I could spend my whole life gathering stories of personal encounters with Jesus and I would still not find the end. People who were raised with Him, people who had never heard of Him until He stepped into their life, people who were raised to hate Him until they encountered Him and His truth, people with every backstory imaginable and more speak of Him changing them. Somehow instead of seeing that for what it is, I let it dilute what it is. The very fact that it is everywhere has made it just an everyday thing I didn't think too much about. I had grown up with it around me, everywhere, so it just was part of life. I couldn't see how deep the words these people were speaking went. I failed to look at the implications of what was said, the possibilities it held for my life. If I had looked closer, I would have been drawn into this love, this life that makes the rest of the world fade into the background.

People want miracles. They fail to be miracles when they happen consistently, then they just become commonplace events and part of life. That is why God's miracles are incredibly personal most of the time. Almost impossible to impart to another person. I can try and tell people about the miracles God is doing in me. It is miraculous to me, because I know where I was, I know what He carried me out of, I know how my heart and mind have changed. No matter how eloquently I describe the process, no one can truly understand what is between He and I. Going through this experience myself, I now understand what other people were trying to convey to me along. What I could not hear before, now rings so deep and true that I don't know why I couldn't see it in the first place.

It is like describing the sunset or the night sky to a blind person, or a song to a deaf person, it doesn't matter how well the words convey the point. Some things can only be fully understood in the experience. This is the experience my entire life has been about. There is nothing that even comes close to it. This intimacy with God that I have found and the knowledge that we will only go deeper in love and closeness is my joy, my hope, my peace, my purpose.

If my words can not fully describe God's goodness and the miracles He has done for me, I must let my life paint a picture of His miraculous goodness. I must live boldly in the blessing. Walking confidently in everything He has given me. I will spread my feathers like a peacock letting the world see the work of the Master.

38:I LIVE IN THE PRESENCE OF GOD

But the path of the just is as the shining light, that
shineth more and more unto the perfect day.
Proverbs 4:18 KJV

God does the most amazing things in the most unexpected ways. If God is doing it, it is almost always something I would have never seen coming, or at least not in the way He does it. He likes to remind us that He sees things in a way we can not imagine, and therefore He can put things together in ways we would've never dreamt of. God has shown me bits and pieces of the future He has for me. He doesn't show me everything because if He did, I still wouldn't see everything. I would see with my human eyes and miss so much. So much of the best parts would look terrifying. Instead He holds my hand and walks with me. As I walk into each step of what He has prepared for me I am able to see it for the blessing that it is. Sometimes it takes a minute. I have to tell my brain to shut up. I remember Who is holding my hand, and then what would've seemed horrible becomes a miracle. God can demonstrate His power and work in me by walking me through what would've crushed me. While he walks me through it he shows me the smile on my face and the peace in my heart the whole time. I am the evidence.

There is a peace and a confidence that only comes from standing in the fire with Him and realizing I can not be burned. He has made me fireproof. There is no fear left for the devil to torture me with. I surrendered everything I am and everything I have to Him.

God connects me to Himself, to life, to everything in the most miraculous way. There is no such thing as alone. When I am without other people, I hear Him the most clearly, I feel Him so profoundly. I am connected to not only Him but He speaks to me of others. Lets me know how I can pray, how I can help, or sometimes how He will move in their lives. God often lets me see what He is doing. He does things for us, He wants us to see them, and be in on the process. Watching Him work in me, and in others brings me a feeling that I do not have a name for.

One evening as I was speaking with God, and I was just flooded with love and a need to say thank you. I told him that I need a better word because thank you doesn't cover it. That was the first word He gave me. He told me to listen. I heard it in my head. Kind of like a shhhing like if I was to sh someone to be quiet, but with a hard K sound at the end, and it repeated shhhkshhk. I tried to say it out loud. He told me not to. Just say it in my head. So I did. When I quieted my mind and just focused on saying that sound. I heard "you are my everything." Along with it I felt that feeling that I was trying to express in giving God my thanks. So now when I tell him thank you I say that instead.

39:YESHA

Jesus, Christ, The Anointed One, Messiah

"This is the work of God, that ye believe on Him whom He hath sent."
John 6:29 KJV

The evidence of God in my life is clear. He shows me my peace when He takes me through a storm. The storm is no longer a thing I fear. He shows me my joy in the waiting. My joy is to simply be with Him. He shows me my self control in the midst of temptation. He is my desire, so I can not be tempted. He shows me patience in any struggle. I don't have to handle things alone. I trust Him in the waiting. He shows me my gentleness when others are abrasive. I have seen what is inside of me, and how He delivered me from it. I will not be angry when others are afflicted. He shows me my kindness when others are unkind. He showed me kindness when I didn't deserve it. He shows me my faithfulness in acts of obedience. He is faithful, so I can be. He shows me my goodness in a broken world. I am different because of Him. He shows me my love in the sacrifices He allows me to make for others. His sacrifice was the ultimate act of love.

40:MY LIFE IS FOUND IN HIM

*No man can come to me, except the Father which hath sent
me draw him: and I will raise him up at the last day.*
John 6:44 KJV

I have been conditioned my whole life to cover certain parts of myself. They are things that belong to me, they are me, I can not change them on my own. I know that they don't belong with me. They are in opposition to what I want to be. I do not know how to separate those things from who I am. So I have two options. I can hide the things and try and pretend they aren't there. This will most certainly end in shame and self loathing. I can accept the things and wear them proudly as just a part of who I am even though they are not meant to be. When I silence my spirit I lose the most important part of who I am. My spirit screams that this thing does not belong, it is not meant for me. My flesh can try to ignore those screams, but there will be continual internal torment.

There is one way to overcome this problem I face. It is by submitting myself to the work that was already done by Jesus. When I let Him in, He shows me how to lay every piece of me at the foot of the cross. He takes the parts that I was never meant to have, the pieces that would destroy me if they stayed. He takes everything. Then He gives me back all of the good things, and when He puts it back He orders it inside me in a way that it can all work together the way it was always meant to. He doesn't stop there. He continues to give me more and more pieces that bring out the beauty in each other. When I give Him what was never meant for me, He gives me what I was always meant to have. He makes me into what I was always meant to be.

41:MELEKH

King

It is the spirit that quickeneth; the flesh profiteth nothing: the words that I speak unto you, they are spirit, and they are life.
John 6:63 KJV

My level of understanding is like ripening fruit. It is able to reach its fullness when I stay connected to the vine. When it reaches its peak God shows me how to use it. If I leave it too long it will begin to rot, and it is meant to be enjoyed. He lets me enjoy the fruit and then shows me where to sow the seeds, so that I can bear more. I am on an adventure with no end. The end of one part can only mean the beginning of another. Each new place He takes me builds me up so that I am fully equipped to experience and enjoy the wonder of the next. His path for me is intentional. There is never wasted time. He uses every piece of the journey for my good.

When I stay in the moment with Him, He explains as we go. He leads me with feelings, words, thoughts, and experiences. When I stay mindful of the present moment, I am always mindful that He is there with me. Now is where I feel Him. When my mind wanders to the future, I can do it with Him, but more often than not it is my mind wandering off on its own. When my mind drifts into the past, I can take Him with me, but more often than not I find myself drifting away. It is in the now where I feel Him. I can look back and see what He has done, and can look forward and think of what He will do. It is in the now that I am fully present with Him.

When I am intentional with my thoughts, when I

understand the importance of where my mind lives, I can begin to live. I had to realize the power in the word of God before I could read it with understanding. I had to realize He is present in my thoughts before I could learn to hear His voice. I also realized I can only be present with Him in the present. I can now be intentional with where I live. Choosing to stay in the present with Him. Trusting that He has shaped my past, and is leading me into a perfect future moment by moment. In His presence is the only place I long to be. He is here now. I will also be here now.

Now is where I am able to listen, to seek. I can not actively participate in the future or the past. I can change how I see them both when I actively participate in the moment. When I let Him shape my now with His words, He reaches into my past and future, making it whole. He touches the eternal things that I cannot. He speaks to my spirit of the eternal and my spirit cries out in praise. The rest of me doesn't always understand but the spirit inside of me is eternal and rejoices at the things He tells me. It is able to comprehend the things my flesh can not. It longs for eternity, for things my flesh cannot begin to comprehend, for Him.

42:LOVE IS THE ANSWER

There is no fear in love; but perfect love casteth out fear:
because fear hath torment. He that feareth is not made
perfect in love. We love Him, because He first loved us.
I John 4:18-19 KJV

There is a fullness in my life I was not aware I had been missing. It wasn't found in any addition to my life it was found in the emptying of myself. When everything in me was removed, I could see what was left. It was beautiful. It was perfect. It was the part of me that is joined to God himself. What I am, who I am, is an eternal spirit. I allowed God to help me pull out all of the clutter I had collected in my mind. It was like cleaning out my closet. There is nothing I can't trust Him with. He knows me better than I know myself. I was able to hand him everything without a second thought. He didn't ask me to waller in it, to relive anything, just to hand it to Him. I could see sometimes what feelings had been stemming from the things I held onto, and feel a release from those torments as I handed them over. He never asked me to think deeply about what we found, I had already spent enough time thinking about it.

It wasn't just things in the past I had held onto it was how I saw my future. How I imagined my future was directly connected to everything in my past. The past had shaped my vision for the future. When I gave Him everything from my past, my vision for the future went with it. Sot here I stood hand in hand with God, holding onto nothing in my past and with no clue what my future will hold. There is no way to describe the freedom in that moment. When He is all that is left, a closeness is formed. I could hear Him more easily than myself. I could see Him, not myself.

This time was not easy. It was the most crushing experience I have ever had. It was also the most fulfilling, hopeful, joyful experience I have ever had. I remember one day driving and It was as though I could just feel God smiling at me in the way a parent would smile at a high school graduation, or a father on his daughters wedding day. It felt like he was proud of me, happy for me, but also this sadness that something was over. I could feel that He was going to miss it. He loves me so much and this part of the journey that I had been rushing through to get to the next step, He had been cherishing the time with me, the closeness. I burst into tears because I was worried I was losing the closeness I had been experiencing with Him. While I still felt that feeling from Him, He was quick to assure me that I would only grow closer to Him. Things would be different but always better. I am always growing and changing and so is my relationship with Him. It can not stay the same, it would lose something if it did.

He didn't leave me in that place without any vision for my future. He began to speak to me of what He is building in me, and with me. Had I been holding on to the past, it would've blurred my vision. God sees me as perfect There is nothing He can not do through me. I let Him remake me from the ground up. Just He and I. My confidence in the future is based on Him. I am confident that He is in me and with me, so I can be confident that whatever He sets in front of me, He will help me accomplish.

Because I know His love for me, I know that the future He has for me is brighter than my wildest dreams. Things I can not even imagine put together just for me with such love and care. In every single step, in every single breath He has included a love note, a lesson, Himself.

43:TSADDIQ

Righteous One

The fear of the wicked, it shall come upon him: but the
desire of the righteous shall be granted.
Proverbs 10:24 KJV

In good things there is an opportunity for evil. The opposite is also true. In evil things there is an opprtunity for good. The greater the good, the greater the opportunity for evil. The greater the evil, the greater the opportunity for good. The choice I have been given, between good and evil, comes with power that I can not possibly understand. The more good I accomplish in each moment, the higher I reach, in that height I must be aware that if I give the enemy footholds he can begin to pull down even the tallest towers. The higher I climb, the further and more terrifying the fall. God would be right there to catch me if I let him, but I do not want to fall if I don't have to.

The deeper I dig myself into a pit with sin and evil the greater the opportunity God has to show me a miraculous rescue. He is even more eager to pull me out of the pit and set me on a mountain, than the devil is to pull me down. Like the pendulum swings with restorative force, so does God. He doesn't pull me back to center where I was, He uses the momentum created by evil for my good. With this knowledge I have hope in even the deepest darkest pit. The greater the hole, the greater the hope.

While I have a choice in every moment, God also could reach in and grab my attention with ease. Sometimes He lets me dig, He lets evil think it's winning, only because He knows exactly how far that pendulum will swing me in the other direction. He could just swing me wherever He wanted. He doesn't have to wait on me to be in a hole. There is something found in that hole though. There is an understanding and a shaping that comes in the rescue. It prepares me for the future He wants to give to me. So God uses evil for my good. He knows exactly how far I can go without being corrupted or broken by the darkness. Then He calls me back and the restoration I experience makes the pain I went through worth it. Looking back at the hardest parts of my life I would easily do them 100x over to get me back to where I am now.

When I hand my life over to Jesus, He gives me righteousness. If I give my life away one piece at a time to sin, I get shame in return. To live in shame is to live in fear and regret. To live in righteousness is to live with the promises of God.

44:YAHWEH-SABAOTH

The Lord of Hosts

When pride cometh, then cometh shame:
but with the lowly is wisdom.
Proverbs 11:2 KJV

One night while I was laying in bed talking with God. He told me He was going to give me a horse. I have ridden horses, I am fairly comfortable around horses, I am in no way qualified to be a horse owner at the moment. I know how to climb onto an already saddled horse that is well trained and ride it around, that is it. He went on to tell me about the horse. He explained that it is going to be my horse and my horse alone. No one else is to touch it. I will be the only one who handles this horse. This will be the only horse I handle. He explained that the relationship that I have with this horse will be incredible. He went on to tell me different things about this relationship I will have that just made my heart leap with excitement. I like horses, but I would have never seen that as something God would give me. I wouldn't have created that desire for myself. I assure you though the picture he painted for me put a burning desire to see it come true.

As we were talking, He said "Do you want to know the name of your horse?". I was kind of stuned, I didnt expxt to find out the name, but YES! Immediately my brain started shooting names at me so loudly it would have been impossible to hear Him. He said "Ok, lets talk about something else, and when you forget about the horse in a minute I will just say the name." So we continued talking and after a little while I just heard "Pinwheel". I said it out loud slightly confused. Pinwheel? I pictured the little foil toy old ladies have in their yards. Ok I know that's God because that is way too random for me to pull out of my brain. I thought about it. A pinwheel operates by the power of the wind, I guess that's pretty cool. God said "keep thinking about it." I began to wonder if there is some symbolism behind a pinwheel. God told me to look it up. So I did.

Pinwheels symbolise spiritual freedom, unseen forces, and childhood innocence. Now I'm grinning ear to ear. I'm wondering how a pinwheel operates, what makes it spin so freely. So I watched a physics video on moment of inertia and rotational kinetic energy. The pinwheel spins so freely because its mass is focused in the center. My mind is reeling with thoughts on how my life flows so freely now that it is centered on God.

God is already using this horse to teach me things and it is nowhere close to being a reality yet. It is in little conversations like this that my faith becomes steel. He shares things to impossibly perfect to be anything but Him.

45: I WILL FOLLOW

Then the Lord put forth His hand and touched my mouth. And the Lord said unto me, Behold, I have put my words in thy mouth.
Jeremiah 1:9 KJV

If I look at the ocean from the land, I see the vastness, I see blue, I see waves that hint at its depth but I can not fully see the ocean from there. The same is true with God's word, and with God Himself. If I look and listen from the shores of unbelief I can get hints of his vastness, but there is no way to experience and understand who He is without diving in with my eyes and ears open.

I have always longed to explore, to see everything I could, to experience all the goodness life has to offer. I know that my idea of goodness is not always good though. I do not know what the experience will be like until I am smack dab in the middle of it. I have often found myself right inside of a situation I was sure I wanted, needed even, only to find out it is nothing like what I thought it would be. There is no amount of wisdom or foresight I can possess on my own that will lead me into the places I want to go without wandering through a lot of places I don't want to be. My life is moving in dimensions I do not see, being pulled by forces I feel but do not understand.

There is a force who wants me to understand Him. He yearns for me to know Him and see His love for me. The others hide in the shadows and confusion. God lights himself up in my eyes. With Him there is no confusion. He makes his character known. I can be confident in one thing, and that is who He is. When everything else is uncertain and terrifying. He is steady, unchanging, and constant. When I allow myself to know Him fully, to trust Him fully, my life becomes an adventure planned out to the last detail by the most trustworthy, powerful, being, that ever was, and ever will be.

He doesn't just lead me through the adventure, He shows me how to live it. He gives me the power to change the world around me. He tells me when to pick something up, and when to put it down. He shows me who to help, and how to help them. He teaches me to listen. He teaches me to speak. He teaches me to love. His heart beats for others. He shows my heart how to beat for others and for Him.

46:MIRACULOUS LOVE

Shall I bring to the birth, and not cause
to bring forth? Saith the Lord:
Shall I cause to bring forth and shut the womb? Saith thy God.
Isaiah 66:9 KJV

I am a six foot tall red head. I love the sun. My skin has never been able to handle it though. My cousins used to joke that I would get sunburnt walking to the car. I suppose standing in the presence of God without the blood of Jesus would be something like me standing on the surface of the sun. When I am full of sin I can not withstand the presence of God. In fact even being near people who reflect Him can be uncomfortable when I am in sin. I want to be near Him, I can feel the warmth. I want to be able to stand in it fully, I just can not in that condition.

Jesus takes my sin so that I can stand in the fullness of God and feel the warmth without the excruciating pain of my own flaws and failures. He lets me know that He has done the same for everyone, so I shouldn't be ashamed. Everyone is standing there by the same grace and mercy He afforded me. As I stand blameless in the love of God, I can look around at my brothers and sisters without shame and without judgement. Some have already been covered by the blood like me and now stand boldly before God. Others still shrink and are hiding behind things for fear of being exposed.

Why would I not boldly walk toward those who still cower

in fear, and lead them out into the bright sunshine? There is no one He can not save. The greater the sin the greater the love shown in forgiveness and the greater the miracle. God is the God of miracles. Not only does He love to perform them, He loves watching me experience them. When I stay in the kitchen with Him I am fortunate enough to watch Him cook them up. Sometimes He explains to me what He is doing, so that when it happens I know exactly how and why. There is a sweetness enjoyed when I have been part of the process that brought it all together, one that I could not experience had I just been blindsided with it.

One day I was in the kitchen fixing myself some toast and coffee. I was grumbling a bit about the waiting, asking for the millionth time if the things He had told me were actual going to happen here in this life. As I fixed my sourdough toast with honey and butter, he told me "add some cinnamon." Immediately I started to try and figure out why. Reasoning that I had once heard cinnamon is good for the metabolism. Halfway through the thought he said "Andrea, put the cinnamon on the toast and go sit down." So I did. I took my breakfast over to the table and as I sat down I could smell the cinnamon coming off of the warm toast. It was almost like every other sense was drowned out for a moment and all I could smell was the sweetness of that honey and cinnamon coming off of the warm crunchy buttery toast. It made me stop. He had my full attention. Then he simply said "Do you think I'm going to let you smell that and then tell you that you can't eat it?".

47: HIS VOICE FEELS LIKE MUSIC IN MY SOUL

"He that is of God heareth God's words."
John 8:47 KJV

There have been times that I have wondered what I will be left with, once everything not meant for me is cleared away. What will I be handed back in return for each piece of me that I have laid at the foot of the cross. I handed Him hopelessness and despair, He handed me hope and joy. I handed Him confusion, chaos, and darkness, He handed me light. I gave Him me, and He gave me Himself. Somedays bits and pieces of the old me try to come back, there is no room for them anymore. I let Him fill me completely. He doesn't leave any space empty in my heart or life. If He did it would be too easy for the very things we cleaned out to come crawling back. Instead He shows me a better way. He shows me a new way to do the good things, and He gives me better things to replace the bad things. There is nothing I can lack or miss when everything is better. I had to trust Him that He wasn't just taking at first. I couldn't see what He was going to do with the empty spaces until they had all been cleared and I was ready to start receiving better. Then one by one, a step at a time, He began to lead me into a better way.

If I had one serious addiction in my life I would say it would be counterfeit love. The kind of love that isn't love at all. Maybe more like lust, jealousy, control, and abuse that are also all very conditional. My heart and soul were desperate for the real thing, but without God's guidance, I very easily and repeatedly fell into the same trap. If I let Him help, He can give me the real thing. The real thing looks almost nothing like what I think. It is so much better. So much so that I wouldn't even recognize it if I saw it.

He begins to show me the real thing, not tell me about it, show me. He is the love I have always been searching for. He is what the hole in my heart cries out for. There is a space only He can fill. My eyes are wide open and watching and listening as He shows me how He loves me every single day. My ears are tuned into Him more than anything else as He tells me how much He loves me everyday.

God is very good at accomplishing many things with every single thing He does. While He is making me fall deeper in love with Him, the hole that was in my heart fills up. He now has the place in my life and in my heart He was meant to fill. He withholds no good thing. He wants me to have a partner and a helper in this life. I ask Him why He won't be jealous of my attention. He asks a question "If you have a husband and he loves you very much. Would you be jealous of his friends? Would you be jealous of his hobbies? Don't you want him to enjoy his life as much as possible?". I think about it. Well the only reason I would be jealous is if he loved any of those things more than me.

God has filled the place He was meant to hold in my heart, nothing can be put above him not even the husband and life I so desire. The way in which He filled that place in my heart was to show me how I should be loved.

48:ABHIR

Mighty One

*Hope deferred maketh the heart sick: but when
the desire cometh, it is a tree of life.*
Proverbs 13:12 KJV

The desires God gives me are not like a pot of gold at
the end of the rainbow. I don't get to follow a path running as
quickly as I can and hope I make it before both the rainbow
and the pot disappear. The desires He gives me are more like
a job offer I accept. If He tells me He is making me CEO of a
billion dollar company and my experience is being a mom, I will
definitely need training. Not only will I need training, I will need
Him every single step of the way because no amount of training
could prepare me to handle that at this point. If He just said
congratulations now run the company, I would probably just
run away. If I managed to stay and try, it would not go well for
me or the company.

When He gives me a job He makes sure it is something I
can not do without Him. This reassures me that He is not done
with me, it reminds me He loves me and wants to draw closer
and closer every single day of my life. There is no end to the
closeness I can have with Him. God has always been with me. If
I don't know how to listen to Him the ways in which He teaches
me are more limited, and therefore the things I can accomplish
are equally limited. He doesn't just throw me into a huge calling
without teaching me how to listen to Him. Once I have learned
to stop and listen to Him there is nothing I can not do. He is
always ready to speak to me. If I don't learn how to quiet my

voice and the voice of the enemy which both sound shockingly similar, then He gets drowned out.

In order to silence these voices, I have to become familiar enough with them to identify them. This means I have to be exposed to them. This is not a fun process. The voices are very difficult to identify when I try to identify them solely by their words. When I recognize emotion instead of words it is easier. Before, when a thought would make me feel panic or confusion I would begin to collapse inside letting it tear me down. Now I can recognize the feeling as part of an attack and not part of me. Just because I feel confused for a moment, doesn't mean I am confused. Just because I feel frustrated for a moment, doesn't mean I am frustrated. I can seperate the feeling from who I am, and then I can calmly follow the logic of the words and decide if they are truth or lie. When I find that they are a lie, I simply use the truth to silence it.

God is so patient and loving He makes sure I am prepared at every step, so that I can walk confidently into whatever He has prepared for me. I do not know if there has ever been anything so difficult as seeing the bright future He promises to me and then having to wait for it. He reminds me that if it were easy everyone would have it. There is a reward for trusting Him. He pays in riches that no man can. When I finally step into that life He has prepared me for, I will do it strong in the knowledge that it is all from Him. He was with me preparing the way before I walked in the door, and He will continue to walk with me every step of the way.

49: I WAS MADE FOR THIS

"The thief cometh not, but for to steal, and to kill, and to destroy: I am come that they might have life, and that they might have it more abundantly."
John 10:10 KJV

Certain foods like potato chips, fried cheese sticks, and churros are such a pleasure in the moment. They can be something to look forward to as well. Once they are gone, sadly, so is every drop of joy. What I am left with is a greasy belly full of regret, maybe a hint of exhaustion, and the need for more usually. This is a type of pleasure that is never satisfied, it is a couterfeit. The more you have of a thing, the more you want, and the more you get, the worse you feel, and the less pleasurable the thing is even in the moment. This type of pleasure is found in something I know is bad for me, or in something good for me that I am using in the wrong way. Either way it is not sustainable and never worth it. Sin is just another word for a counterfeit version of a good thing. That is why it is so attractive to me. It promises to fill a very real desire that was put into my heart by God himself. The counterfeit version only leads me in the opposite direction of what it claims. When I deny God, I also deny the good things He wants to give me. I am not capable of creating them on my own. I have a very real enemy who seeks to destroy me by feeding me counterfeit desires that lead to my destruction.

There is only one way, Jesus. Without him, I have no

access to the father and to the blessings and desires I so desperately crave. It isn't complicated. He made it easy for me. All the hard part has been done. Trust Him, seek Him, listen to Him and the rest falls into place, maybe painfully sometimes but it is always worth it.

50: I AM HIS

*"My sheep hear my voice, and I know them, and they follow me:
And I give unto them eternal life; and they shall never perish
neither shall any man pluck them out of my hand. My Father,
which gave them me, is greater than all; and no man is able to
pluck them out of my Father's hand. I and my Father are one."*
John 10:27-30 KJV

How do I explain the intimacy and closeness I have with someone I have never seen with my physical eyes, I have never heard with my physical ears. Faith is my only method of communication. It gives my eyes the ability to see what I could not, and my ears the ability to hear what they could not. Without faith I would have to silence the sights and sounds that were not verifiable by others, or believe that I had gone insane. I would not have had the courage required to jump into to day long conversations in my head with God. What I did have was enough faith to believe if I actively sought Him, He would make himself known.

When I sought Him he answered, it didn't start out as a voice with distinguishable words. It started out with a telephone call and a glimpse into a future that could be mine. The feeling that God was about to show me his goodness and how much he loved me. Then in twenty seven four leaf clovers, after I asked to find one. Every time I opened my eyes to the possibility that He was speaking to me, I saw that He was. Until eventually, I was able to hear His voice in my thoughts aside from my own. Sometimes he just gives me large amounts of information to process. Most of the time it is just He and I speaking like I would with anyone else.

When I stop and think about our time together, it takes my breath away and makes my heart skip a beat. All the times He has woken me up in the night just to show me something whispering "come on get up for a minute, it will be worth it." Every morning He is there waiting for me to wake up. He walks with me through each day sharing every moment. He is there with me as I fall asleep. There is no way to describe a relationship like this. He knows me completely. He loves me completely.

51:GOD MAKE ME BRAVE

*But, the word is very nigh unto thee, in thy mouth,
and in thy heart, that thou may doest it. See, I have set before
thee this day life and good, and death and evil;
Deuteronomy 30:14-15 KJV*

The world is full of hurting people. The pain is no respecter of income or status. It is in every geographical location. It doesn't care if I am young or old, beautiful, or disfigured. This pain floods the earth. The pain comes with its own doctor, one who deals in ways to anesthetize the spirit. The pain and the doctor go hand in hand. Without the pain, I would not need the doctor. The ways in which the doctor gives me to numb are very temporary. They require constant use and never actually heal the pain. They also steal my ability to function as a whole, they block the pain, but they also block my thoughts from coming to fruition, my spirit from being able to move within me, and keep me in a sort of constant confusion.

The doctor had come in and given me drugs for a pain I was never brave enough to even recognize. I live in a world where we have something to handle every discomfort. If I am feeling tired, I must need caffeine. If I am feeling restless in my thoughts, I eat or watch TV to quiet them. If my mind keeps leading me in a direction that makes me uncomfortable, I pull out my phone and lead it somewhere else. There is no end to the ways in which I can silence my inner thoughts.

One day I got sick of being numb, so sick I prayed that

God would set me on fire for Him. Let me burn for Him. He pointed my heart to His word. Then He gave me a desperation. That desperation made me want to pour every last drop of faith I had into the power of His word. The power of His word did not disappoint. It began to clear the confusion in my mind with a burning fire for Him. Before I even realized what had happened God showed me what He had done. I was fully alive and burning for Him in a way I never knew possible.

52: FIREPROOF

The fining pot is for silver, and the furnace
for gold, but the Lord trieth hearts.
Proverbs 17:3 KJV

There is a pain, and confusion in the middle of the fire, that cannot be explained. I have handed over my life to God. God is kind and gentle and stays with me through it all. He reminds me that I am in a spiritual battle, and that He is with me. I still have to sit through it. It feels like everything around me is spinning out of control. The only constant is Him. He is gravity. He holds me together, He holds it all together. When it feels like even time is speeding up and everything is spiraling out of control, I draw close to Him. The closer I get to Him the more time starts to slow, and the spinning becomes stillness. He holds me and everything else falls away. When I let myself get lost in the spinning confusion, it starts to speed up the more I look at it, He calls me back. Without Him there would be no way. I would be lost. I see that. I feel that. I know that. It is in this knowing that my faith is refined, that my trust in Him is made strong, and the foundation of my very existence is poured.

I feel His pain as He watches me struggle through. I know what I am feeling is nothing compared to what He felt in my place on the cross. What I feel is just enough to show me who He is and what He has done for me. It brings me close to Him. I would do it every day for the rest of my life if that is what I needed to do to stay close. I don't know how long I need to stay in each battle, I don't know how many battles I will go through. I know I will never ask for Him to take me out early, and I will never ask for Him to keep me from the battle. I asked Him to set a fire in my heart. I asked Him to let me fight for Him. I asked for Him to let me come into eternity with Him victorious. He answered.

53: WHERE MY TREASURE IS

When thou sittest to eat with a ruler, consider
diligently what is before thee:
and put a knife to thy throat if thou be a man given to appetite.
Be not desirous of his dainties: for they are deceitful meat.
Labor not to be rich: cease from thine own wisdom.
Wilt thou set thine eyes upon that which is not? For riches certainly
make themselves wings; they fly away as an eagle toward heaven.
Proverbs 23:1-5 KJV

I like to take my girls to the fair each year. We all enjoy the rides, and the food. The whole place is a sort of exhibition of indulgence. When cheese isn't enough by itself, we wrap it in bacon and breading and pickles and stuff it in a donut or something. The rides get taller and faster and flashier. The boats and RV's and hot tubs get fancier. There is no shortage of things to marvel at. We get the mega ride pass every year so we have unlimited rides.

One year after a few corn dogs my middle daughter, Bella, rode a super fast spinning thing I can not even begin to describe. After she got off she said she felt a little woozy. She insisted she needed to go ride the swings that raise up in the air and spin in a big circle. I tried to tell her if she was feeling woozy she probably shouldn't, but she was dead set that the air would help her. So we climbed on the swings. They lifted up and started spinning. She is sitting behind me. As we are flying around 40 feet in the air, I hear a puny "mom". I turn around and she is green. There is nothing I can do. I tell her to just breathe. She manages to hold it together until the spinning stops and as soon as she stands up out of her swing, she blows. Then she vomits again on the way to the trash can and then more in the can. She looks miserable. The other girls stay with my mom who is with us. She and I have to cut the trip short and head home.

I have found myself in the same situation as Bella more times than I care to admit, well the same but different. On vacation with an unlimited drink package, spending money on things I will never use, overeating at a restaurant until I feel sick, the list could go on for a very long time. I think the problem that I had the most trouble with was the way I treated my time. I have given away my life one minute at a time to things that promise fullfillment but never fullfill. It is easy to go to a store and spend $200 on earrings, or a purse, or makeup. How many hours of my life did it cost? When do I realize that more new clothes, toys, makeup, junk food, random amazon buys, subscriptions, kids activities, pet toys, or whatever, have actually made me a slave? My entire life spent trying to earn these things that can never fullfil me. Then leading my kids to believe this is what happiness looks like and therefore raising them to be slaves as well. Jesus broke the bonds of my slavery and gave me freedom. If I enjoy the luxuries this world affords it will be a surprise blessing from God, not because I sold my life one hour at a time to receive it.

54: HE REJOICES IN ME

My son, if thine heart be wise, my heart shall rejoice, even mine. Yea, my reins shall rejoice, when thy lips speak right things.
Proverbs 23:15-16 KJV

My life lately feels like I'm on a deserted Island. There is one palm tree and about fifteen feet of beach. That is it. Luckily I am not alone on the island. God is with me. Yes, The God. I know that I'm going to be fine. He has assured me I will not lack anything. In the morning He makes sure I have my tea with all the fixings, later my coffee with cream and breakfast. I have plenty to eat and it is all good. The only thing is, I don't see any of it until I'm ready to enjoy it. There is no fridge where I can loiter and graze mindlessly. There is no abundance of foods to choose from. I don't spend lots of time deciding what to make. I use what he gives me for that meal. It's always delicious. In fact I eat better on this desert island than I did back at home with a stocked pantry and fridge. I also enjoy the food so much more when it comes at just the right time.

It takes some getting used to. At first it was hard not to worry, sitting on the beach with only a palm tree. God is with me, but I can't see Him. I know He is here though because He speaks to me in my thoughts. He also provides for me at every turn. He has alot of opportunity to show me He is here. He has to provide every snack and every meal, and all the conversation on the island, it is just He and I after all.

It turns out this island is a sort of training camp. While He has me alone and free from distraction He is helping me to build my spiritual muscle. At the same time He pours His wisdom into me. The closeness I get to experience with Him shows me His character and love. Being able to live so closely wrapped in His love gives me a confidence and strength I didn't know I could possess. He assures me I won't be on this desert island forever. He has big beautiful plans for me. He just has to make sure I'm ready for them.

55: LET ME KNOW HIS LOVE

My son, eat thou honey, because it is good; and the honeycomb, which is sweet to thy taste: So shall the knowledge of wisdom be unto thy soul: when thou hast found it, then there shall be a reward, and thy expectation shall not be cut off.
Proverbs 24:13-14 KJV

Sometimes the candy in the candy store that looks so fun to a kid turns out to be a big disappointment. I remember taking my daughter to a candy store for her birthday one year. She saw this giant beautiful swirly lollipop. It was enormous it looked like something you would see in a movie. She insisted that was what she wanted. We bought it and she got it home and decided to try it. She was so excited. When she tasted it she looked like the wind got knocked out of her a little bit. It just had that plain lollipop flavor, kind of like hardened sugar. She was not impressed.

I have learned in life that more often than not, I do not know what I really want. Even after 44 years I still frequently think I want something in my life only to later realize what a mistake it either was or would've been.

Part of the problem has always been that my view of myself was completely distorted by the baggage I carried. I couldn't see past my mistakes, the way other people had treated me, and what the world tells me is good. Once I handed all of that stuff over to God, He began to show me how He sees me. As someone who has a hard time taking a compliment, this took some getting used to. He sees me as perfect.

The love He has for me is greater than I can fathom. He loves every single part of me. He knows all the freckles. He numbered every hair on my head. He's seen the stretch marks. He loves it all. Every part of me means something to Him. He wants me healthy. He wants me happy. He promises to never stop helping me grow and mature. He loves me completely just as I am. He sees my heart, my wants, the way my mind works. He laughs with me. His heart breaks with mine. He feels joy when I do. Often when I feel this overwhelming love for Him stir up in me, He tells me what I feel is just a reflection of the way He is feeling looking at me. I feel just a small portion of the love He has for me and it moves me to tears, to laughter, to sing, to just stand in awe.

56: FATHER

Rejoice not when thine enemy falleth, and let not thine
heart be glad when he stumbleth: Lest the Lord see it, and it
displease Him, and He turn away His wrath from him.
Proverbs 24:17-18 KJV
If thine enemy be hungry, give him bread to eat; and if
he be thirsty, give him water to drink: For thou shalt heap coals
of fire upon his head, and the Lord shall reward thee.
Proverbs 25:21-22 KJV

When I look at animals it is easy to see that each type of animal has a particular set of instincts built in. Cats behave very differently from dogs. Chihuahuas behave very differently from golden retrievers. Every animal has a unique role they play. God has given me dominion over the earth. He has given me authority and therefore responsibility.

When my girls began to get old enough to leave home alone, I would put my oldest daughter in charge. The first time I explained that she would be in charge when I left she got very excited and puffed up looking over with a smile at her sister. Her younger sister looked like things were definitely falling apart in her life. Until I explained what it meant to be in charge. Bella was complaining that Sophie would use her newfound authority to boss her around and make her do whatever she wanted. I asked Bella if I was in charge when I was home. She said yes. I asked her if I made her go get me snacks and clean up after me. She said no. I asked her if I was the one who made her the snacks and cleaned up after her. Suddenly the smile switched from Sophie to Bella, and Sophie's wind went into Bella's lungs.

I know as a child of God who has been given authority

and a command to live like Jesus, that I am not meant to live my life like an animal. I am held responsible for my time. I am given the responsibility of living a life of service. In everything I do I should do it as though I am doing it for God. Just like when Sophie was left in charge of the house every mess she picked up, everytime she helped her sister, she was doing it for me because I asked her to. So when I take care of what I am given in this life, and most importantly when I take care of my brothers and sisters I am doing it for God.

57: I AM WHO
HE SAYS I AM

It is not good to eat much honey: so for men to search their
own glory is not glory. He that hath no rule over his own spirit
is like a city that is broken down and without walls.
Proverbs 25:27-28 KJV

The first thing Adam and Eve did after they ate the fruit in the garden was to hide because they were naked. The fruit told them that something was shameful about their nakedness. God did not see anything wrong with their nakedness. They were living exactly as he had created them to. This seems to be Satan's biggest play, poisoning pure and good things and using them against us.

Anytime I have heard the voice of condemnation and judgement it has been his. God corrects me by showing me a better way. Satan just shows me that the things I do are evil and wrong. He tries to point out my flawed motives at every turn. He tells me I am a mistake, and my very existence is a blight. It is my job to recognize the voice is from him and counter with my paid in full receipt from Jesus.

Yes, I am a work in progress. I am still forgiven, loved and God promises to perfect everything that concerns me. He also says that He sees me in my perfect state already. He is outside of time. He sees me as I will be when the work is complete. Loves me fully from the very beginning. Just like I love my newborn baby not only in that moment, but I love it because I see a future for it I see what it could become. God doesn't just have a dream of what could be, He knows what I will be.

When I make my life about Jesus, He gives me an identity in him. He gives me the opportunity to serve Him. He shows me how to push back the darkness in the world. He shows me how to be His hands and feet. He leads me to places where I can find purpose. He gives me a calling and then helps me to fullfill it.

The enemy wishes nothing more than to destroy my identity. He wants me blind and confused and unsure of who I am or what I am capable of. If I don't know where I belong or the authority I have been given, then I am left believing I am powerless. I would remain twisted and crippled by lies if not for the love of Jesus. He finds me, He shows me who I truly am. He shows me who I belong to. He builds me up with a love that changes everything. In Him I find my identity, my hope, my life.

58: THE WAY, THE TRUTH, THE LIFE

Whoso keepeth the fig tree shall eat the fruit thereof:
so he that waiteth on his master shall be honored.
Proverbs 27:18 KJV

The sky still makes my jaw drop in awe every day. It may be a sunrise, sunset, just a bright blue mixed with fluffy clouds, storm clouds, or the night sky. Something so big and unchanging that changes absolutely every moment of every day. The more I get to know God, the more I think He is like the sky. He is always moving, always changing, but constant at the same time. He is what He is. His character stays the same. The way He moves and appears changes throughout the day and night and seasons.

This keeps me in awe of Him even more. I never know what He will show me from day to day. Whatever it is, I know it will be good. When I say good I do not always mean happy and pleasant. I mean that He is good and He is with me. I trust Him to guide me through whatever may come. He can show me the brightest sunniest day, or the eye of the wildest hurricane. Either way it is an adventure and a sight to behold because I am with Him.

He shows me how to walk out into the world with confidence. He gives me eyes to see beyond what I used to see. He gives me a heart for the people around me. When I walk through life with Him, it's like getting a behind the scenes tour of life. I don't just see things, He gives me wisdom in every experience.

The wisdom He gives is a source of joy and peace that cannot be found anywhere else. Something I can not help but want to impart to others. Engaging with people and being able to share what He has given me is an incomparable joy. Somehow, He never runs out of ways to shock and inspire me. He leaves me in awestruck wonder every single day.

59: NEVER ALONE

The wicked flee when no man pursueth: but
the righteous are as bold as a lion.
Proverbs 28:1 KJV

There was a point after being broken down to nuts and bolts and then put back together, where God spoke to me and told me He wanted me to walk confidently. I had always breezed into every situation in my previous life with the confidence of someone backed by God. I had been leading my own way back then, and so leading myself into one dead end situation after another. I did it with the confidence of someone who has been rescued by God at the end of every dead end. I was tired of dead ends.

I let God show me a new way. In order to see the new way, my old way had to be completely destroyed. Now I am walking with new sight. I see but its through the eyes of faith. I hear but its with the ears in my spirit. This means seeing with my physical eyes but looking past what I see, to what God is showing me. I still hear what the world is telling me, but I have to push it to the side and quiet my mind so that I can hear what God says. He shows me how far I have come. I am out on the rink skating, away from the side. Sometimes I start to feel pretty good about how I am doing. The skating rink is pretty empty though. I know that more people on the ice changes everything.

It is the fear of falling that keeps me wobbly. This is where He reminds me that it is a good day for things to go wrong. He isn't just a teacher, He is my God. There is nothing He can not do. He promises He will not let me hit the ground. There is no unpredictable circumstance, no move I make, that He has not already foreseen. He is there waiting at the end of every leap and with me in every turn. I hear His voice. I see Him move. He is urging me to trust Him, to move confidently even though I feel like I will fall. He will catch me and have me back on my feet before I ever hit the ground. Not only that but every time He gets to catch me, it just reminds me He is there. He builds my confidence with every fall.

60: HE REMOVES
THE THORNS

He that covereth his sins shall not prosper:
but whoso confesseth and forsaketh them shall have mercy.
Proverbs 28:13 KJV

It is a different kind of love. God tells me He knew me before I was born. He formed me in my mothers womb. He put me exactly where I needed to be and with who I needed in order to shape me into what I would become. All of the things that I have experienced have shaped me into who I am at this very moment. He knew it would all happen. Some things He allowed, some things He did himself. All of it working together brought me where I am. He looks at me knowing everything, knowing far more than I could ever know about myself. He tells me He loves me completely.I am precious to Him beyond what I can conceive.

Some of the places I hold inside are painful. He knows. He says He has been waiting for me to give them to Him so He can turn all the pain into something else. He turns pain into purpose. He tells me I am stronger than I realize. There is nothing I can not accomplish with Him. He tells me there is nothing He would not do for me.

61: THE UNSEEN SHALL BE SEEN

A faithful man shall abound with blessings:
but he that maketh haste to be rich shall not be innocent.
Proverbs 28:20 KJV

There is one thing I have always fully believed in, even as a child. The name of Jesus. My parents had always told me of the power in holding that name in your thoughts, or crying out to Him. My mother lived in Jamaica for a time when she was growing up. Her parents were missionaries there. She told me about how deeply spiritual the people of that country were. They believed in the unseen as much as the seen. They would perform voodoo ceremonies and rituals frequently. They recognized the darkness there and celebrated it in some ways and deeply feared it in others. In recognizing the darkness and communing with it they afforded it power in their lives.

My grandparents job as missionaries was to show them a better way. Show them a way out of the fear and darkness they had been surrounded with. To show them the light. Because they already believed deeply in the unseen and the powers that moved around them, they were able to pick up the Bible and read it with a faith that had already strengthened. Their faith had been misplaced in the darkness but it was there and it was strong. As soon as their faith was turned to Jesus, the darkness had to flee. The brightness in their life He replaced it with was all the more evident.

The great lie most of the world suffers from now is the

lie that God does not exist. My whole school life I was taught to trust only what I see with my eyes. What can be verified by others. If it can't be verified, it isn't real. Then came the continual news and tv that shaped my view of the world. This was to be trusted because I could see it with my eyes. The way my heroes in movies thought and lived were what I was to admire and seek out. Not only that, but anyone who deeply believed in Jesus and the things of the Bible were made out to be uneducated and lower class. It has always been acceptable to have that surface level church mentality, as long as your regard for education is higher. This is how the enemy blinded the faith of generations.

It is easy to turn my faith from the unseen that is darkness to the unseen light. What is more difficult is becoming fully aware of the unseen when all of my faith is in what I can see. When I look at the world with eyes wide open and aware of the forces at work. The plan of the enemy was so obvious. He made us to believe in only what we could see, then created a world where He could control exactly what everyone saw. I see that world turning on its head now. We are able to use the same tools he brought to distract us and blind us with His lies. I see individuals showing the truth they see, rather than buying into His lies. The truth spreads like wildfire. His darkness and lies crumble in the light of truth. The battle lines become more clearly defined every day with God's truth as a guide.

62: AS I WAS MEANT TO BE

And ye know in all your hearts and in all your souls, that not one thing hath failed of all the good things the Lord your God spake concerning you; all are come to pass unto you and not one thing hath failed thereof.
Joshua 23:14 KJV

I feel like a tiger that has been raised in the zoo. I have been given food and water and my physical needs have all been met. I have never experienced what my life was meant to be. I have only known the toys the zoo gave me, and to be fed at certain times. I have always had a safety in my enclosure, trusting that the people running the zoo are looking after my best interest. In exchange for my freedom, I am given what looks like security but is actually a prison.

Until God stepped in, and opened my cage. He lead me out into the world. A world I had no idea even existed. A world full of Him, full of wonder. In order to live in this new world I need Him. If He just released me on my own, I would cower in fear and go running right back to my cage not knowing how to survive. Not only does He lead me out He invites me to come with Him. As we walk He shows me things and tells me about the wonderful world that exists outside of the zoo.

He knows exactly what I was born to do, He knows exactly where He should take me. He has a place all prepared for me out in the world. One where I can grow and become the tiger I was always meant to be. He gives me a life in exchange for my cage.

He tells me about this life He is leading me into as we

walk. My mind can only hold on to bits and pieces. I can not understand what joy awaits me in living with Him, in walking into a life fully designed by Him. I try to guess and look forward to it as we walk, He reminds me I can not think big enough. The plans He has for me that the biggest parts my mind can hold on to are actually the smallest pieces. So I trust in who He is, every step we take together He shows me more and more. I cannot fully comprehend what He is walking me to, but I know it is a future brighter than my wildest dreams. More fulfilling than anything I could've ever imagined and most importantly a future where I am drawn closer and closer to Him each day. When my eyes are focused solely on Him I move quickly and confidently toward all the goodness He has spoken over my life.

63: HE MAKES ALL THINGS NEW

I am weary, O God; I am weary, O God, and worn out. Surely
I am too stupid to be a man. I have not the understanding of a man.
I have not learned wisdom, or have I knowledge of the Holy One.
Who has ascended to heaven and come down? Who has
gathered the wind in His fists? Who has wrapped up the waters in
a garment? Who has established all the ends of the earth?
What is His name, and what is His Son's name? Surely you know!
Every word of God proves true; He is a shield to
those who take refuge in Him. Do not add to His words,
lest he rebuke you and you be found a liar.
Proverbs 30:1-6 ESV

Some days I wake up feeling defeated. I know I am not. There is a defeated feeling that comes when life is all to familiar, the days begin to bleed together. In routine I can wander through my day without much effort. My mind and body are accustomed to each task and can do it on autopilot. In the unfamiliar, I am stimulated and forced to move in new directions and operate in new ways. This takes confidence. If I am stepping in fear, listening to the voice in my head, one that says each step takes me closer to catastrophe or failure, the unfamiliar becomes the impossible. If I am walking with God, I am confident. I know there is no such thing as impossible. What looked impossible before, now looks like an opportunity to demonstrate His greatness and power. Problems turn into blessings, anxiety into adventure, and defeat turns into victory. He changes the outcome in my mind before I have ever set foot into the battle.

I have no idea how to live a life of adventure, in the unfamiliar every day on my own. I know it is what I long for desperately. I also know what I am capable of both good and bad. Life is not an adventure meant to be lived on my own. It is an adventure meant to be lived side by side with God. Where every moment, every breath, can hold revelation and newness. There is nowhere He can not take me, nothing He can not show me, and He has already proven there is nothing He would not do for me.

So when the defeated feeling starts to creep back into my day or my life, I need only look to the one who walks with me. I know it is only a matter of time before He speaks and moves and makes all things new.

64: AS I AM

Favor is deceitful, and beauty is vain:
but a woman that feareth the Lord, she shall be praised.
Proverbs 31:31 KJV

What if what was inside of me started to become visible on the outside? If what I carried around in my heart and mind began to take form in my physical appearance, I would most certainly be forced to evaluate what was inside me. As I allow God to change my heart I begin to see changes in my physical self and the world around me. At first the change I see is because He has given me new eyes to see with. I see myself as He sees me. I see myself as what He has called me to be. The old image I have of myself begins to flake away like an old layer of skin. A new image is born, one that is founded in the fact that I am His.

Before, I had seen myself as never enough. The harder I worked to exercise and eat right, to build my body into the image the world tells me is desirable, the more I lost myself. There is a beauty in being me as God created me that cannot be found any way other than through Him. I have a uniqueness that God has given me, that is where my beauty lies. The more I try to look like someone else, the more I deny the God given beauty I have.

He gave me a dream one night. I was walking down a busy street when a group of very sophisticated people ran up to me and stopped me. They began telling me how beautiful I was, they went on and on. It felt really good. They told me I needed to come with them so they could help me reach my full potential. They took me upstairs in a skyscraper. There were beautiful models walking around everywhere. They continued to tell me how remarkable my beauty was, it was a feeling I had longed for my whole life without even realizing it. Something inside of me had been chasing approval like that. We got into a large room where they all pulled out charts and pencils and markers and began marking on my face and body all of the areas they can improve. They were creating a list as they went. My confidence quickly turned into self loathing. I began to realize how old I was, my skin didn't look like all the other girls, it needed help, I was larger than the other models. They continued to point out flaw after flaw, until I realized nearly every part of me would need completely changed in order to meet their standards. Even then, it would never be as perfect as the younger women who seemed to meet that standard on their own. Then I looked around again at all the other women who had at first glance looked so confident and beautiful and I could see a sadness, a hollowness. They were so weak they might has well have been puppets on strings.

That is when I woke up. I asked God what that was all about. That is when "Priceless" began to play in my head again. "I see you dressed in white, every wrong made right, I see a rose in bloom, at the sight of you, Oh so priceless." He whispered "you are perfect. I love you."

65: IN THE BEGINNING WAS THE WORD

For the word of God is alive and active,
sharper than any double-edged sword,
it penetrates even to dividing soul and spirit, joints and marrow:
It judges the thoughts and attitudes of the heart.
Hebrews 4:12 NKJ

When I can see the work I need to do in front of me it is easy for me to take off on my own and accomplish things. This gives me a feeling of confidence, but my confidence gets placed in the wrong person. When I think I see a clear path forward it is very difficult to keep myself from running ahead of God. His pace is different than mine. In keeping me in the dark, He has helped me to learn to walk at His pace with Him. The longer He keeps me here the more accustomed I become to the pace at which He moves. I begin to recognize myself speeding up now instead of just feeling like I am at my usual pace.

The earth has a gravity of it's own, it is always trying to pull me towards it. It constantly screams for my attention. The closer I stay to God the stronger His pull is on me and on my life. His pull is different than that of the earth. His pull requires me to focus on Him. I must constantly choose to ignore the pull of the earth and instead look to Him. He doesn't stop calling me back to Him. He persists, He rescues. I want more than just continual rescue. I want to follow Him where He wants to take me.

66: I WILL SPEAK LIFE

"Be not afraid, but speak, and hold not thy peace:
For I am with thee, and no man shall set on thee to hurt
thee: for I have much people in this city."
Acts 18:9-10 KJV

I live in a world consumed with worry, it always looks for the problems. The miracle of being a mother is probably the greatest joy I have been afforded in this life. From the beginning though the world begins to turn our focus to problems. We are only allowed a brief moment of happiness in the knowledge that a new baby is on the way, before the testing begins. We begin to check for any and every possible problem. Most of the tests, I was never asked if I wanted, they just do them. Then there were tests that were more invasive that they would have liked to do but I refused. I remember asking them exactly what we were testing for, it was usually some sort of horror that would result in the death of the baby or a life trapped in its own prison of a body. When I asked what they would do if the test came back positive, would they be able to save the baby or help it's condition, the answer was no. They just wanted me to be prepared if the baby died or had permanent disease or injury.

When I am focused on a possible negative outcome, I miss the beauty of whatever is in front of me. Not only that I am prone to throw away a gift based on fear, rather than to wait and see it through trusting God to make whatever comes into my life a blessing. How many dreams are abandoned before they ever begin, how many moments of wonder and anticipation are squashed by worry and anxiety? Why would I ever give my time and energy to worry when I know God is in charge, He is good, and He loves me? I choose to guard my thoughts. When the devil whispers what ifs, I speak of God's goodness, mercy, and faithfullness. While the world is focused on the problems, I am focused on the opportunity for God to move and work.

In a world that screams worry and fear constantly, I will choose to speak hope and life. In a world that speaks only of imminent destruction and doom, I will speak of God and His unstoppable power and unending mercy.

67:UNDENIABLE BEAUTY

But know that the Lord hath set apart him that is godly for Himself:
the Lord will hear when I call unto Him.
Stand in awe, and sin not: commune with your
own heart upon your bed and be still.
Psalm 4:3-4 KJV

When I think of the word torture, I see a midevil dungeon with the hooks and racks and knives. It may seem like the world has evolved past that, I assure you it has not. The torture has gotten even more diabolical and effective. I do not have to be qualified a conspiracy theorist to know that governments have been openly using psychological warfare and torture for a very long time. The mind is where torture truly takes place. The enemy has known this from the beginning. That is why the first attack on humanity was one that took place inside us. I do not presume to understand the full extent of what that apple did, but I know whatever it was it changed the way we think and perceive.

His methods have not changed. He still seeks to destroy me in my thoughts. This is one reason it is so very frightening and difficult to listen for God at first. The enemy also has a voice in my thoughts. Without being aware of what is transpiring in my thoughts, I would either be forced to ignore my thoughts all together, or go mad listening to them. Either of those options end in destruction. God wants me to be aware that I am involved in a spiritual battle and that it takes place in my thoughts. When

I am aware of the parties involved in this war, I can make myself aware of the thoughts in my mind without fear. Confident in the voice of God I listen with enthusiasm and delight. He gives me authority and truth to shut down the voice of the enemy. When I am free to converse with God in my thoughts, anything becomes possible.

68: SET APART

Therefore, thou art inexcusable, O man, whosoever thou art that judgest: for wherein thou judgest another, thou condemnest thyself; for thou that judgest doest the same things.
Romans 2:1 KJV

People are capable of remarkable things when they put their minds to it. The physical feats we witness from professional athletes look like they are done with such ease and grace that it might be possible for us. Standing at the top of a high dive staring down at the water it feels different. Some people are able to live life with the same grace and effortlessness. I tend to stand at the edge of each morning like I have been thrust into an olympic high dive competition and never learned to swim. It is in this feeling that God's grace is able to abound. When I recognize my own shortcomings, and allow God to step in with grace, He is able to take every area I give Him and replace it with His strength. Because I have been so humbled by life, I see myself as one big short coming. There is not one area I want to maintain control of.

I am well aware that I am unqualified to fix myself. If I see myself as unqualified to fix myself, how could I ever see myself as qualified to fix anyone else? What I have been qualified to do is point people to the One who fixed me. I have been given a testimony in the process of being made new. I cannot tell anyone how to fix themselves, I can share how God fixed me.

69: I AM PRECIOUS IN HIS SIGHT

*But he is a Jew, which is one inwardly; and
circumcision is that of the heart, in the spirit, and not in
the letter; whose praise is not of men, but of God.*
Romans 2:29 KJV

I am not a huge sports fan. I did enjoy watching my kids play though especially when they were very small. They are innocent and unpredictable, there isn't much care for winning or losing, they are just learning to pay attention to the fact that there is even a game in progress. I remember one particular game where a boy found a half eaten pickle on the field during the game and stopped what he was doing in order to pick it up and finish it. Watching the game at this level is never about who wins or loses, it's about watching your child. Hopefully they are having fun and learning to pay a little bit of attention to what is going on.

When my daughter was small I remember there were certain players that right from the start had speed and a natural ability to focus and play. They were somewhat entertaining to watch and it was always nice to win. The player though that I remember most fondly was one that would frequently turn into a bird of some sort, or dinosaur out on the field. She would trot awkwardly flapping her hands and squawking. She was tiny, with giant glasses and had almost no interest in the ball or the game, but she had so much fun. I remember one day as my daughter ran past I hollered at her that she was doing great keep it up or something like that. The little birdie heard me and ran up to me with those big eyes under those big glasses and the biggest grin. She said "what about me? Did I do good?" My heart melted into a puddle and I wanted to take her home with me. I told her she was doing great. She beamed proudly and flapped back onto the field.

In my walk with God, especially after a more difficult day when I feel like I might be falling behind or failing. I come to him and ask, am I doing good? He reminds me of that little girl with the big glasses on the soccer field. The pressure instantly fades, I smile remembering He sees my heart, and that He adores me.

70: WHERE THERE IS WATER THERE IS LIFE

He staggered not at the promise of God through unbelief; but was strong in faith, giving glory to God; and being fully persuaded that, what he had promised, he was able also to perform. And therefore it was imputed to him for righteousness. Now it was not written for his sake alone, that it was imputed to him; But for us also to whom it shall be imputed, if we believe on Him that raised up Jesus our Lord from the dead; Who was delivered for our offenses, and was raised again for our justification.
Romans 4:20-25 KJV

God created me to live fully. To hold Him in my heart, to walk with Him, to be His. He is not a sloppy designer. He never rushes His work. He created me in such a way that I would be capable to fullfill my purpose. He designed every step, every detail, down to the last microsecond, the last hair. When He created the world, He had to create things capable of holding life inside. Everything He made was good. All perfectly designed to reflect Him to hold pieces of Him. He is our source.

I am in a place right now that is incredibly uncomfortable. It is difficult to make it through the day sometimes. God asked me earlier if I believe He can make me comfortable in the place I am now. Yes, of course He can. There is nothing He can not do. Then He reminded me that if I am uncomfortable right now, it is because I need to be. I am not in trouble. I am not sinning or being ungrateful by feeling unhappy with my life. It is simply the place I need to be at the moment in order to accomplish what

He is accomplishing in me, and in my life. This helps me think bigger than my feelings. I still feel uncomfortable, I still long for change. I can recognize those feelings though and knowing they are accomplishing His purpose in my life helps me to tolerate them.

When I keep my faith in God, and not in what I feel or see, then I am stronger than any obstacles or doubts I may come against. I recognize Him at work in my life. I see that everything I am going through is working toward the purpose He has called me to. I do not falter when I get tired or weak or uncomfortable because I know He is in charge and He is capable of finishing what He started in me.

71: EVERYTHING UNDER THE SUN

Therefore being justified by faith we have peace
with God through our Lord Jesus Christ:
By whom also we have access by faith
into this grace wherein we stand,
and rejoice in hope of the glory of God.
And not only so, but we glory in tribulations also: knowing that
tribulation worketh patience; and patience, experience; and experience,
hope: And hope maketh not ashamed; because the love of God is shed
abroad in our hearts by the Holy Ghost which is given unto us.
Romans 5:1-5 KJV

By entering through faith into what God has always wanted
to do for us- set us right with him, make us fit for him- we have it all
together with God because of our Master Jesus. And that's not all: We
throw open our doors to God and discover at the same moment that
He has already thrown open His door to us. We find ourselves standing
where we always hoped we might stand- out in the wide open spaces of
God's grace and glory, standing tall and shouting our praise. There's
more to come: we continue to shout our praise even when we're hemmed
in with troubles, because we know how troubles can develop passionate
patience in us, and how that patience in turn forges the tempered
steel of virtue, keeping us alert for whatever God will do next. In alert
expectancy such as this, we're never left feeling short changed. Quite
the contrary- We can't round up enough containers to hold everything
God generously pours into our lives through the Holy Spirit!
Romans 5:1-5 MSG

It has been what feels like a lifetime since I have been able to enjoy television. It used to be a comfort, an escape. Now when I try to watch something, everything just feels unwatchable. I can not identify with the characters, they might as well be aliens living on a different planet. Last night I was too mentally tired to write or read. My thoughts were not flowing and I just felt exhausted but not in a way I could sleep. So I turned on the TV to try again. After attempting a few different movies, I finally found one that my daughter joined me to watch. It was a popular new childrens movie. I began to get interested in the show. It started to feel like when I used to watch TV. I was relaxing and escaping to somewhere else.

I watched with her for the whole two hours until the movie ended. After the movie had ended, I felt different than I have for the last months. I was relaxed, my mind was in a different state. The movie had somehow drawn me back into a comfortable state for a bit. I told my daughter goodnight and started to get ready for bed. This comfortable state was the most uncomfortable thing that had happened to me all day.

I was no longer moving at God's pace. I was moving at the pace of the world. There is a certain comfort in the pace of the world, my mind and body relaxed and numb. It is a superficial comfort though. It reminds me of the matrix. I can have one pill and remain numb inside what is not real, or I can wake up and see what is underneath. I have chosen to look at what is underneath the comfort. There is no peace in the comfort this world affords. There is distraction, there is numbing, there is temporary happiness even. I don't want it.

I will gladly take the discomfort of being aware that I am an alien in this world. It is not my home. I am walking with God as a traveler here on my way to something better. If I never fully relax into this life, good. If that is what it takes to push me into growth and change and action, then so be it. The discomfort keeps my eyes on peace, on Him. The discomfort means I am different.

I do have joy, peace, and hope. I continually feel the love of God in my life. I have passion and purpose. I would trade the comfort this world affords for those things in a heart beat. The comfort this world affords is hollow. The peace from God is real and unshakeable.

72: LET ME BE KNOWN BY MY WORKS

So here is what I want you to do, God helping you: Take your everyday, ordinary life- your sleeping, eating, going-to-work, and walking-around life- and place it before God as an offering. Embracing what God does for you is the best thing you can do for Him. Don't become so well-adjusted to your culture that you fit into it without even thinking. Instead, fix your attention on God. You'll be changed from the inside out. Readily recognize what He wants from you, and quickly respond to it. Unlike the culture around you, always dragging you down to its level of immaturity, God brings the best out of you, develops well-formed maturity in you.
Romans 12:1-2 MSG

I beseech you therefore, brethren, by the mercies of God, that ye present your bodies a living sacrifice, holy, acceptable unto God, which is your reasonable service. And be not conformed to this world: but be ye transformed by the renewing of your mind, that ye may prove what is that good and acceptable, and perfect, will of God.
Romans 12:1-2 NKJ

In the movie Pirates of the Caribean, there were pirates that belonged to Davy Jones ship. When they first came aboard the ship they looked like normal human pirates, after some time they started to resemble parts of the ocean until eventual most of them looked like coral and fish and had almost fused to the ship in a sort of grotesque way. The world had done the same sort of thing to me. After 44 years I had taken on alot of the characteristics of the world and I was beginning to fade into the background. I had spent quite alot of time and energy trying to make myself look more like what I thought the world wanted me to look like. The better I got at it, the less I looked like myself.

One day I looked in the mirror and realized I could never transform myself enough to satisfy the image I had in my mind of what I should look like. So I fell on my knees and asked God to take what was left of me and do something with it. He didn't tell me I had gone to far, and done too much damage. He did the opposite. He opened His arms and assured me that nothing had been lost. He wouldn't let one second of my pain and life go to waste. He moved in with a restorative force and everything that had looked bad in my life, He turned for my good. Just like that swinging pendulum, He used the force of my swing in to darkness and the world, to pull me back the other direction to Him. Then He showed me how to draw closer and closer to Him. The closer I draw to Him the more I am pulled to Him. When I remain in His gravity the pull of darkness cannot reach me to pull me back. Instead, He continually pulls me closer and closer.

I let God remove the parts of me that have grown out of the world. What I am left with is a pure version of myself. In this untarnished me, He is reflected. His reflection displayed in the magnificent work He does in me. There is nothing more uplifting and humbling than this.

73: A LIGHT IN THE NIGHT

*And lest I should be exalted above measure through the
abundance of the revelations, there was given to me a thorn
in the flesh, the messenger of Satan to buffet me, lest I should
be exalted above measure. For this thing I besought the Lord
thrice, that it might depart from me. And he said unto me*

*"My grace is sufficient for thee: for my
strength is made perfect in weakness."*

*Most gladly therefore will I rather glory in my infirmities,
that the power of Christ may rest upon me. Therefore I take pleasure
in infirmities, in reproaches, in necessities, in persecutions, in
distresses for Christ's sake: for when I am weak: then I am strong.*
II Corinthians 12:7-10 KJV

I shed my old self like a locust leaves a shell. It stays in
the past a reminder of the transformation I have undergone. It
is dried and dead and left behind no longer a part of me. When
I listen to the testimony of other people they show me their old
shell. It is the evidence of change. If I only see the new person
walking around, the change is not as evident. When they point
to the shell that they were, God's work is undeniable.

The proof of God is everywhere, if I look for it. Thousands
of years worth of these testimonies documented. Personal
miracles abound every day all of the world. It only takes enough
faith to open my eyes and ears to what people for millenia have
been shouting. Countless personal encounters with God. The
very fact that the world chooses to ignore this is proof of dark

forces at work. Proof of the dark forces only prove further that God and his goodnes are indeed real and present.

Sometimes it is in pain I find purpose. It is in loneliness I find the one who knows me better than I know myself, loves me in a way no one else can, and promises to be with me always. It is in my grief I find His peace. His humility and grace disolve my selfishness and pride. My insecurity and anxiety are no match for His love.

74: NOTHING COMPARES

Love suffers long and is kind
Love does not envy
Love does not parade itself, is not puffed up
Does not behave rudely
Does not seek its own
Is not provoked
Thinks no evil
Does not rejoice in iniquity
But rejoices in the truth
Bears all things
Believes all things
Hopes all things
Endures all things
Love never fails
I Corinthians 13:4-8

The things God shows me sometimes remind me of an Easter basket. Every year I take time to put together Easter baskets for my kids. When they were smaller a giant chocolate bunny was an important part of the basket. I knew that the bunny was hollow and the chocolate tasted more like wax than anything, but it is what they got excited about so I made sure to stick one in each basket every year. As the girls got older they began to care more about the quality and type of candy rather than what it looked like.

As I mature in Christ, the things I ask for change. I am learning that real joy and purpose in this life doesn't come in the big showy packages I used to long for. Instead the sweetest pleasures usually come in smaller bites hidden in the basket. They are not in the house I live in, the car I drive, or the vacations I take. Instead the sweetest pleasures come in the revelations I receive from God and the time I get to spend talking with Him each day. Some days He sends someone into my life and allows me to encourage them, or share Him. His greatest gifts are not the ones the world sees but the ones He gives me in secret.

Everything I could ever need or want is found in Him. He doesn't just provide what I think I want, He knows what I want more than I do and then provides. He carefully curates each day with such love and attention that the way He feels about me is undeniable. In every single thing, I see His love, His attention to each detail. He leads me through the darkest battles, the deepest pain, the greatest joys and incredible revelations. He does it all and in every type of moment His love surpasses all else. It is greater than anything I can ever face. I know this because I have faced the unthinkable while surrounded by His love. I have been in the fire and never burned. I have walked on the waves and never sank. I have stood in the brightest sunshine and seen His love shine brighter.

75: FAITH OVER FEAR

We don't yet see things clearly. We're squinting in a fog, peering through a mist. But it won't be long before the weather clears and the sun shines bright! We'll see it all then, see it as clearly as God sees us, knowing Him directly just as He knows us! But for right now, until that completeness, we have three things to do to lead us toward that consummation. Trust steadily in God, hope unswervingly, love extravagantly. And the best of the three is love.
I Corinthians 13:12-3 MSG

There is a rush I get at the top of a steep waterslide, or on the edge of a high dive. I have to force every step and every breath. I know that I am safe, it will be fine. Fear tells me to turn back at every step, but there is a satisfaction in acting in the face of fear. Something built into me has always known fear is something to be defeated. After the jump, after the slide, after I am safe on the ground the fear is replaced by relief and a heightened sense of safety and well being that is worth far more than the price of the initial fear.

This is how it feels to go all in with God. In order to experience being held by God, I must leap into His arms and let go of what I'm clinging to. Fear tells me to turn back with every breath. The closer I get to the edge the greater my resolve to jump. Once I jump, it's too late to turn back so fear is shown for what it is, useless. Fear might scream at me from time to time, but it's too late I couldn't turn back now even if I wanted to. I can't unjump off the high dive. This is where fear loses all power over me. It is in this moment, God's voice is the clearest. He tells me He has me, and to keep my eyes on Him, not the ground below or where I lept from. When I look at Him time slows, the

ANDREASISSONS

falling turns to stillness, and it is just He and I.

76: I WILL WALK IN TRUTH

Pursue love, and desire spiritual gifts, but especially that you may prophesy. For he who speaks in tongues does not speak to men but to God, for no one understands him; however, in the spirit he speaks mysteries. But he who prophesies speaks edification and exhortation and comfort to men. He who speaks in tongues edifies himself, but he who prophesies edifies the church. I wish you all spoke with tongues, but even more that you prophesied; for he who prophesies is greater than he who speaks with tongues, unless indeed he interprets, that the church may receive edification.
I Corinthians 14:1-5 NKJ

People are born desiring greatness. We are called to adventure and to push the limits from the beginning. The world gives us things that look similar to what we are seeking but they never satisfy us. I see entire generations of boys that have been consumed by video games. The world told us there is danger everywhere so we sent them into a virtual one. Now we have men who feel powerless and useless in the real world. The basic skills and confidence that would have been developed instead became an addiction to instant gratification and the lures of a fictional reality.

Girls are similarly locked safely inside and forced to live in a virtual world. Their world is full of social media, youtube videos, and games of their own. They spend their days idolizing fictional characters, and searching for ways to mold themselves into the images they see. Girls with no self confidence become mean. The hurt and insecurity they feel on the inside turns outward, or they turn even further inward with self harm.

The evidence is clear that fear pushes us to destruction when we let it lead. Character and lives are developed and molded when we live in spite of fear. I cannot walk blindly into the world denying danger exists. I cannot send my children blindly into danger either. I walk into the world in wide eyed wonder side by side with my God. He guides me through some things, and around others. With Him I can walk boldly anywhere. I can be an example for my children, showing them how to live boldly. When the rest of the world cowers in self doubt and fear of the unknown, I must be a light shining with confidence. When the rest of the world screams out in spiritual blindness at one another, I must remain calm and steadfast in the knowledge that everything is in His hands. I must be the evidence of adventure, greatness, and something better.

The adventure God provides in this life is a supernatural one. He moves in ways the world cannot understand. He moves in me. My adventure may not look like an Indiana Jones movie, but it feels like it sometimes, only better. God gives me spiritual gifts to be used. He gives me the Holy Spirit to move in my life in powerful and undeniable ways. Each day I uncover more of the mystery that surrounds me. God doesn't want me in the dark, He wants me seeking Him so that He can show me the beautiful miracles that surround me every day. He wants to let me in on the adventure. The same power that raised Jesus from the dead is alive in me, not to be ignored but to be wielded. I am not left powerless, I am given the power to achieve great things in His name.

77: NO WEAPON FORMED AGAINST ME SHALL PROSPER

Be anxious for nothing, but in everything by prayer and supplication, with thanksgiving, let your requests be made known to God; and the peace of God, which surpasses all understanding, will guard your hearts and minds through Christ Jesus.
Philippians 4:6-7 NKJ

As I lay in bed this evening walking with God. I was feeling sort of defeated, tired, frustrated because I can not see any relief in sight. I am in a very uncomfortable season. A thought popped into me head "whatever happens tonight just remember I love you." I countered with something like "what the flip." The thought had come through my head like get ready for this one you are not gonna like it. Which immediately sent me to a place of fear. Then I remembered God hasn't given me the spirit of fear. That fear started to dissipate.

Then God asked if I would like another word to think about. So he gave me the word to say in my head. I repeated it until I started to see what looked like a soldier on a ship. Then I saw me sledding down a hill laughing, then I was sliding down a giant slide. Then God said to think about it. He started to explain that I was headed into battle but had forgotten. In my mind I was on a sled sliding down a hill. I can not head into battle with that mentality.

I thought about it further. Then I began to wonder if

the "whatever happens I love you" thought was from God. I wondered if I would be facing something tonight that would challenge or frighten me. Again I started to become afraid. Then I remembered again. God does not give me the spirit of fear. So I pictured myself going into battle. What that would look like. How would God want me to ride into battle. I know He is with me. I pictured the warriors of the old testament going bravely into battle with God on their side. So I pictured myself riding into battle. Then I began to wonder what I would face tonight. So I began to picture the most frightening things coming into my room and over me. Dark things I could not possibly fight on my own. Then it made me angry. I remembered I have the power of God in me and I saw an image of me standing on my bed shooting fire out of my eyes and mouth and destroying the thing.

I recited my favorite verse in my head "He who justifieth me is near, who can contend with me. Let us stand together. Who is mine adversary? Let him draw near to me." The fear had been replaced with a desire to conquer and defeat. The powerless feeling of being stuck had been replaced with victory.

Then God showed me how my thoughts and attitudes had changed once I recognized that I was in a battle. The demons I was fighting were attacking me with the feeling of powerlessness and being stuck. I just needed to become aware of the battle that I was in. Maybe fire didn't shoot out of my eyes and mouth, but it might has well have because those feelings that had me defeated turned instantly to victory.

78: BOUNDLESS LOVE

Summing it all up friends, I'd say you'll do best by filling
your minds and meditating on things true, noble, reputable,
authentic, compelling, gracious- the best, not the worst; the
beautiful, not the ugly; things to praise, not things to curse.
Put into practice what you learned from me, what you heard and
saw and realized. Do that, and God, who makes everything work
together, will work you into His most excellent harmonies.
Philippians 4:8-9 MSG

"'Turn your eyes upon Jesus, look full on His wonderful face." That song is playing in my head at the moment. I long so desperately to see the face of Jesus. To be able to picture it as I speak with Him. I have heard testimonies of people that have seen His face. It seems that at this point in my life it is not something I am allowed to see. When I ask why, I am told that it has to do with faith, and I can not understand everything right now. I can't complain. If I had to choose between seeing Him and hearing what He has to say, I would choose His voice everytime.

Still as I stare up at the ceiling in conversation with Him, my mind tries to create an image sometimes. It never holds. I can not even imagine it as hard as I try. He often tells me "Andrea, there is nothing I would not do for you." When He says this to me, I know it is from Him, I know it is true. I feel it in my soul. When I contemplate those words it leaves me breathless. I also know when He says that, what comes with it is there is nothing I would not do to protect you, even from yourself. So while I have the backing of almighty God completely, it leaves me wondering what do I do with that knowledge.

First of all the sense of security, confidence, and love

it brings are worth mentioning but indescribable. After my head stops spinning with the implications of the statement. I recoginze that when He says that, He is reminding me to ask Him for the things I need and want. The needs are all covered He has assured me of that so while there are things in my life that still need handled, He has told me to view them as already done. I just have to wait for the appointed time. The wants fall into the same category. I don't need to keep asking for what has already been done. So what does that leave?

There are plenty of people that I know that need things, that I would like to see blessed. I learn to start praying for people outside of myself and my immediate household more often. I already did this some, but it was usually when God would put them on my mind. I used to wonder why I would need to pray because God knows what they need better than I do. Then one day I prayed for someone. It was a man a barely know from church. God put him on my heart though. I didn't know what to pray so I just prayed God bless him in a big way. Then I forgot all about it. Until later I had heard that he had been given a very nice car. God reminded me of my prayer. I do not fully understand how and why things are the way the are. I do know that when God put the man onto my heart and had me pray for him, then blessed him in front of me later. It strengthened my faith and gave me great joy.

There is another reason to ask God for something. This one seems most obvious but it is the reason that gets overlooked most. Why do I not ask God to help me understand my feelings of helplessness or powerlessness or defeat more often in a direct way? I am very good at complaining about how tired I get in the battle, and how I am feeling defeated. Why do I not directly come to Him and ask for help here? I suppose this is a good opportunity to ask Him to help me with all of that right now. Prayer is simply put, a conversation with God. I do it all day long. I will start taking Him up on His offer more by facing the feelings that are afflicting me head on, and then asking Him for help with them. I realize He may not remove the feeling or the situation but I know He is always willing to help me get a better perspective and to walk me through each situation. He says there is nothing He would not do for me, I will give Him every opportunity to show me.

79: PREPARE MY HEART TO RECEIVE

You can be sure that God will take care of everything you need, his generosity exceeding even yours in the glory that pours from Jesus. Our God and Father abounds in glory that just pours out into eternity. Yes.
Philippians 4:18-20 MSG

God has put a desire in my heart to move, to travel. More than that, He has made me incredibly uncomfortable in the place I am. I ache for change, to move, to be moved. I am still here. He takes me through each day and makes it new as He speaks to me and changes me. My physical surroundings do not change. I imagine this is alot like being led through the wilderness. I know He isn't keeping me here. I am with Him, so I know I am taken care of and I wouldn't want to be anywhere else. I also do not want to stay here.

I have talked to Him about it. Apologized for my attitude, asked Him to help me fix it. He has explained that I am not supposed to be comfortable in the wilderness. I am supposed to trust Him. I am doing that. I have not turned my eyes anywhere else for comfort. I do not try and lead myself out of the place. I want what He has for me, not what I can find on my own.

He reminds me that if I was comfortable where I am now, it would be very hard for me to leave it. I would not want to move. Change is hard, really big change can look impossible. So I sit with Him, and I wait. He doesn't just give me the change I ask for, He prepares my heart to receive it joyfully. He wants the things He gives me and the purpose He has for my life to be seen as the beautiful gift it is. His mercy isn't only shown in what He gives me, it is also evident in how He gives it to me. Not one second of my time does He leave untouched with His love.

80. AN OCEAN OF GOODNESS AND MERCY

"When thou art bidden of any man to a wedding, sit not down in the highest room; lest a more honorable man than thee be bidden of him; And he that bade thee and him come and say to thee, give this man place; and thou begin with shame to take the lowest room. But when thou art bidden, go and sit down in the lowest room; that when he that bade thee cometh, he may say unto thee, Friend, go up higher: then thou shalt have worship in the presence of them that set at meat with thee. For whosoever exalteth himself shall be abased; and he that humbleth himself shall be exalted."
Luke 14:8-11 KJV

I always dread the end of summer. It means life will resume it's full pace again. Then one day very late in the summer, the air changes, and I see a few leaves begin to fall. Suddenly I remember the good things in fall. I can open my windows to the outside air again and feel the breeze. Everything begins to start again but there is a fresh energy now. I am reminded of how good change can feel. God gave day and night, different seasons, and different years so that I can experience life with fresh eyes and renewed energy. He does the same thing with seasons in my life. I can feel when a season must be at an end. I can also feel the anticipation of the next season.

The seasons in my life are different than the season of the earth. I do not have a calender that shows me when to expect the transition. I do not even know what the next season will be unless God chooses to reveal it to me. So I hold on to what I do know. God is good and He loves me. He promises to perfect everything that concerns me. When I look back at the evidence of my life, He has always been there, He has never failed me. He has never left me. He makes all things for my good.

There is something wildly exciting about walking into a new season of life with absolutely no clue what to expect. It would be terrifying but I know who created the seasons, and He walks with me. As I enter this new place, I do it humbly, realizing I did not lead myself here, nor do I know what is in store for me. I carry a grateful and hopeful heart while keeping my eyes on Him.

81. BABY STEPS

"He that is faithful in that which is least is faithful also in much;
and he that is unjust in the least is unjust also in much."
Luke 16:10

The darkness seeks to extinguish the light before it is born. It wants to kill hope before it can be formed. It seeks to keep me focused on the horror, despair, and failures of the world. When I become captivated by the darkness, the light looks different. Instead of seeing it as a bright hope, it shines a light on my life and I can not help but look inward in horror. So it feels painful, and irritating.

When I let light replace my darkness I become a part of the hope. Now when I see the light in others, I feel an instant connection and kinship. Our lights combine to shine even brighter. This is even more irritating to those still in the darkness. When I stand in the light looking out at people still stuck in the darkness. I don't feel judgement, or anger, even when they are outwardly irritated with my very existence. Instead, I feel the same kinship and closeness I felt with my brother or sister walking in the light. I was also in the clutches of darkness. Having lived through a miraculous rescue, I can point at the shell of my old life showing others there is hope. I can share my testimony without shame because the condition of my old self only further proves the miraculousness of my rescue.

When I walk faithfully in obedience with God through my rescue, I show that I will also walk faithfully in obedience with God through the battle. When I walk faithfully with God through the battle, I know I can walk faithfully with God into what He has promised. God makes each step I take clear. I faithfully take each step one at a time, following Him. Soon I look around and realize He has led me into a new life and a new calling, preparing me all along the way.

82. HUMBLED TO BE EXALTED

My heart rejoices in the Lord;
My horn is exalted in the Lord.
I smile at my enemies,
Because I rejoice in your salvation.
No one is holy like the Lord,
For there is none besides You,
Nor is there any rock like our God.
Talk no more so very proudly;
Let no arrogance come from your mouth,
For the Lord is the God of knowledge;
And by him actions are weighed.
The bows of the mighty men are broken,
And those who stumbled are girded with strength.
Those who were full have hired themselves out for bread,
And the hungry have ceased to hunger.
Even the barren has born seven,
And she who has many children has become feeble.
The Lord kills and makes alive,
He brings down to the grave and brings up.
The Lord makes poor and makes rich;
He brings low and lifts up.
He raises the poor from the dust
And lifts the beggar from the ash heap,
To set them among princes
And make them inherit the throne of glory.

For the pillars of the earth are the Lord's
And he has set the world upon them.

He will guard the feet of His saints,
But the wicked shall be silent in darkness.

For by strength no man shall prevail.
The adversaries of the Lord shall be broken in pieces;
From heaven He will thunder against them.
The Lord will judge the ends of the earth.

He will give strength to his king,
And exalt the horn of his anointed.
I Samuel 2:1-10 NKJ

If I am away from home and one of my daughters calls me hungry, she wants a pizza. I agree to order pizza and have it delivered to her. The pizza comes and the daughter who called me gets it from the driver and brings it in. The other girls smell pizza in the house and they are hungry too. The first daughter takes it all to her room quickly and keeps it for herself. I come home and the two daughters who didn't get any pizza are hungry and cranky. The first daughter is still in her room with a bunch of leftover pizza. She doesn't even come out because she knows what she did was wrong.

I take the two hungry daughters out to eat for a nice dinner, then to see a new movie, and then we go for ice cream afterwards, while the other daughter hides in her room with her cold pizza. Had the first daughter come out and apologized, I probably would have let her come too, but she hid in guilt and shame.

God wants to bless all of His children, above and beyond what we deserve or expect. When He blesses me, I must remember it is not because I deserve it more, it is because He loves me unconditionally. When I recognize blessings as a gift from Him, rather than something gained of my own merit, it makes me want to share His goodness with my brothers and sisters. When I focus solely on what He is giving me and see it as something I have earned, or something that belongs to me I become greedy and miss out on so many other blessings He has to give.

If I do succumb to my nature and to my flesh, I must remember that Jesus has paid the price for my sins, all of them. When I turn to him in repentance, He graciously welcomes me back with open arms. At any time and from any position in life, God can take back what He has so graciously offered, or He can restore and rebuild me to heights I could've never dreamed. When I choose to put my faith in Jesus, I am humbled, and God exalts. When I put my faith in my own merits, God removes His hand and allows me to try on my own. Despite what the world often looks like, God is in control. He chooses when and who to lift up, and when and who to bring down. In everything, He is just and perfect.

83. I GROW IN CHALLENGES

But the spirit of the Lord departed from Saul,
and a distressing spirit from the Lord troubled him.
I Samuel 16:14 NKJ

Sometimes my thoughts feel like bare feet on hot concrete. When my thoughts start to feel like this, I have learned to lean into God. He slows me down, and makes me brave. Then I separate myself from the emotion the thoughts are bringing. I remind myself that God is in absolute control, if He is letting me experience this, it must be for a reason. I slow down and look at each thought as it comes. When I stop to look at the thought, without fear of where it will take me, it loses its power over me. I can follow any thought with confidence knowing that I have the Holy Spirit to guide me and remind me of the truth.

Sometimes I feel like even my brain is inflamed, I get overwhelmed with irritation. Every sound in the house, clank of a dish, people talking, any disturbance of the silence feels like a megaphone in my ear. I can easily recognize this is not a reasonable way to feel. There is something else causing my irritation other than the actual sounds. God allows me to feel this way sometimes to prepare me for when I go out into the world and encounter real irritations. If I can control my reaction when I am alone in my room, it will help me to control my reaction out in the world.

When I learn to see the frustrations and thoughts that plague me some days as training, I can face them with confidence and a smile. If I maintain the view point that it is just pointless torment, it becomes intolerable. God only allows my frustration and suffering if it is going to be used for my good. When I suffer, He suffers. He also trusts me to be brave, and knows that I find joy in being able to overcome. If He just handed me everything on a silver platter, I couldn't share in the victory. He wants me to share in the victory, and enjoy my life and my eternity as more than a conqueror. It is in the difficulties that victory is earned not just given.

84. MADE TO WORSHIP

Regarding angels he says:
"The messengers are winds, the servants are tongues of fire."
Hebrews 1:7 MSG

There is something found in the presence of God that I do not have a word for, when I don't have words to describe something, I ask God. He gives me a word to repeat in my head until meaning comes. I was thinking about how it feels to sit looking up toward God and feel Him looking back at me. When I can feel His gaze, I feel His emotion, I don't have words to accurately describe this feeling. He gave me a word. This is the meaning that popped in my head: To be in His presence is to worship Him, to worship Him is my purpose, I delight in my purpose.

When ever I had heard the word worship I always pictured singing maybe people on their knees with their hands lifted. I know this is also worship. Until recently I had not realized that simply being concious of God's presence with me is worship as well. When I carry Him with me throughout the day, I devote my every move to Him. My heart can not help but try and please Him. The amazing thing is it doesn't even have to try. God is pleased with me. He loves our talks, He loves the way my heart cries out to Him when I have a problem or a joy. He loves it when I recognize something is from Him and gaze up with a smile in wonder. The relationship we have is the most natural and easy thing I have ever experienced. I simply exist in the knowledge of

Him, and He allows me to reflect His emotion, His wonder, His love. Even in the hard parts of life, the relationship I share with Him is perfect and natural. It is the most sacred part of me.

I live a life surrounded by mystery and wonder. I am surrounded by angels. I am flooded with the Holy Spirit. I am in constant communion with God. There are forces of darkness that seek to destroy me but cannot because of the supernatural protection God gives to me. This life is anything but boring when I open my eyes to the reality of God's word.

85. I GUARD MY THOUGHTS

Unto the pure all things are pure; but unto them
that are defiled and unbelieving is nothing pure; but
even their mind and conscience is defiled.
Titus 1:15 KJV

There is a childlike wonder that lives in me. When I allow it to come out, it fills me with joy. When I take my kids to the park and begin to play with them like a child, this part of me starts to come out. It doesn't come naturally at first, I have to begin to play and then I begin to enjoy it. If I don't put in the initial effort to see the park like they do, then I go with tired eyes that have been there a million times and would rather sit on a bench on my phone or be at home. It isn't just the park where this is true.

I have realized that I have to put in a little effort to view the world through the eyes of faith and wonder. Somedays I am just tired, and when I don't see the results of what I have been faithfully working toward in my life, it is hard to keep moving in faith. When I get up anyway and start to move with determined faith, it isn't long until my thoughts and feelings start to follow my actions. The initial effort I put into moving when I don't feel like it, comes back to me multiplied. God sees me pushing through exhaustion and complacency. Some days He lets me start out full of energy and momentum, other days I have to work a little harder to get going. I trust that He is always with me and when I give what I have, He is faithful to step in and do the rest.

86. SIN IS DEFEATED

For verily He took not on Him the nature of angels;
but He took on Him the seed of Abraham.
Wherefore in all things it behooved Him
to be made like unto His brethren,
that He might be a merciful and faithful high
priest in things pertaining to God,
to make reconciliation for the sins of the people.
For in that He Himself hath suffered being tempted,
He is able to succor them that are tempted.
Hebrews 2:16-18 KJV

The world is full of places that take my breath away. Giant redwood trees, white sand dunes that feel like ice in the heat, giant underground caverns, country side with winding dirt roads and leaves ablaze in red, orange, and yellow, incredible seascapes, mountains, and deserts. The beauty and glory of God's creation speak to me. He put it here for all of us to experience and enjoy. It is easy to get used to the natural beauty that I live in every day.

There is a feeling I get when I experience some new natural wonder for the first time. I am reminded that there is more in the world than where I have made my home. There is still something to be seen and experienced beyond the comfort of where I live. It is the same way with my spiritual life. When I step out of my comfort zone, and I allow God to show me new ways of doing things, He reminds me there is more to life He wants to show me. He never runs out of ways to amaze and inspire.

There is a newness He puts in every single day. It is

nothing short of miraculous. When I invite him into the moment, He takes it and turns it into something else. He gives me that feeling of walking into the redwood forest for the first time. When I am conscious of Him in the morning, He starts my day with the excitement and anticipation I would have as I'm about to head off to the airport for an adventure. Somehow He does it in such a way that every single morning feels different, even when they are the same.

The world wants me in a rut. It wants me chasing unattainable things. It tells me to work harder so that I can finally go on a trip and have that feeling, or buy the new car and feel that newness for a moment. Trips end, and even if they don't, endless traveling eventually loses its newness. The new car soon becomes just my car. The feeling of newness and adventure the world provide are fleeting. I purchase those moments with my time. I become a slave to my desires.

God makes every single moment new, He requires everything. When I give Him everything I am. He gives me my freedom. He frees me from the desires of the world. He gives me a life full of what my heart has always been searching for, Him.

87. SURROUNDED

For He shall give His angels charge over
thee to keep thee in all thy ways.
Psalm 91:11 KJV

When I read the word of God, I believe every word is true. It is not meant to be looked at as a puzzle that only the most brilliant minds can solve. If the word says it, God means exactly that. It goes even deeper than just the literal meaning, it always goes deeper. The literal is true as well though. When God's word says a chariot of fire came down and took Elijah up to heaven, that is exactly what happened. I believe there is symbolism involved beyond just the literal action that took place, but the starting point is that He actually rode a chariot of fire to heaven. When the bible says Jesus died on the cross to defeat sin and death, His body laid in a tomb for three days and then He rose again. That is exactly what happened. It is far more complicated and beautiful than the surface level value of those words, but it is true literally first. God's word is incredible. It is true on every single level. There is no end to the depth. I could study my entire life and never run out of new truths.

One day as I was reading about Elijah and how He prayed God would open His servants eyes to see. Then he saw the angels and fire surrounding them. What a sight to behold, how incredibly confident and powerful He must have felt. I began talking to God about the angels. We have talked about them before. I know I have angels around me. I asked God if He would open my eyes like Elijah's, so that I could see the angels around me. He simply responded "you do not want that." I thought about trying to eat my toast in the morning or do school with the girls and seeing things surrounding me. Then I tried to picture these beings. I know that I am not capable of imagining what I would feel should I see them. Then my mind went further. If my eyes were opened to see the angels, I would also see the fallen angels. I am pretty quick to think I am tough and can handle things bravely, until I am face to face with something that requires me to be brave. I am so thankful that God knows what I want, because I rarely do.

88. EVERYTHING IS FOUND IN HIM

The angel of the Lord encampeth round about them that fear Him, and delivereth them. O taste and see that the Lord is good: blessed is the man that trusteth in Him. O fear the Lord ye His saints: for there is no want to them that fear Him. The young lions do lack, and suffer hunger: but they that seek the Lord shall not want any good thing.
Psalm 34:7-10 KJV

God is the ultimate multitasker. When He created the earth, He joined beauty and function in ways that demonstrate His ability as creator. In each tree we have beauty, shade, fire, shelter, air, homes for countless living things, and more. He doesn't just create physical things that way He creates moments, thoughts, spirits, if it exists it is because He created it. This means if it exists, there is a way it was designed to fit into His creation. There is a purpose it serves.

Thunder, lightning, sunshine, tornadoes, and even sickness have a purpose. There is nothing in His creation that is beyond His control. If it is still here, He is using it to serve a purpose. When sin entered the world, things changed. I do not know why that tree was in the middle of the garden, or why the serpent was allowed to be on the earth. I do know God can not be surprised. In my experience it is in pain that I can clearly see purpose, if I am brave enough and humble enough to really look. In the most agonizing moments of my life God has showed me most clearly the why. It goes beyond the strength produced by pain, beyond the need to cultivate free will. There is a depth to creation that I know I am incapable of comprehending.

While I can not know the why of everything, the things I am capable of understanding, God lovingly and faithfully explains when I ask and listen. He makes His character known in each moment. I am assured that my life is in His hands. I know that His hands are always working for my good, so I can be confident in joy and pain. I know that I am always moving in the right direction when I am moving closer to Him.

89. THE ONLY WAY

And I heard, as it were, the voice of a great multitude, as the sound of many waters and as the sound of mighty thunderings, saying, "Alleluia, For the Lord God omnipotent reigns! Let us be glad and rejoice and give Him glory, for the marriage of the Lamb has come, and His wife has made herself ready." And to her it was granted to be arrayed in fine linen, clean and bright, for the fine linen is the righteous acts of the saints. Then he said to me "Write: Blessed are those who are called to the marriage supper of the Lamb!" And he said to me, "These are the true sayings of God." And I fell at his feet to worship him. But he said to me, "See that you do not do that! I am your fellow servant, and of your brethren who have the testimony of Jesus. Worship God! For the testimony of Jesus is the spirit of prophecy." Now I saw heaven opened and behold a white horse. And He who sat on him was called Faithful and True, and in righteousness He judges and makes war. His eyes were like a flame of fire, and on His head were many crowns. He had a name written that no one knew except Himself. He was clothed with a robe dipped in blood, and His name is called The Word of God. And the armies in heaven, clothed in fine linen, white and clean, followed Him on white horses. Now out of His mouth goes a sharp sword, that with it He should strike the nations. And He Himself will rule them with a rod of iron. He Himself treads the winepress of the fierceness and wrath of almighty God. And He has on His robe and on His thigh a name written:

King of Kings
And
Lord of Lords

Revelation 19:6-16 KJV

It is my perspective that determines the outcome of my life. The perspective of many people today is that man is ultimately in charge of His own life. This is a very simplified way to put it. It shows in alot of different ways. People have put their faith in science and the powers of this world. There was a time when the science that we let govern our lives could be comprehended by anyone who wanted to invest a little time into understanding it. That time has passed. The science that now governs the world we live in is so complex and vast that there is not one person on this earth who can comprehend every area fully. I doubt there is one person on this earth that fully comprehends their single area of expertise. So people choose to blindly put their faith in a science they have no hope of fully understanding. In a perfect world maybe this would work. One where the people involved in learning were dedicated only to the pursuit of truth and the betterment of lives. This is not the world we live in. The world we live in is controlled by people who live for money and power. They recognize that the way to control the world is through the religion of science. Studies are manipulated, scientists are silenced when their findings disagree with those powers, and the truth never reaches the light of day. What we have instead are lies sold as truth. So today when I put my faith in science, I am actually putting my faith in the very corrupt powers of this world.

Another option I have is to recognize the spiritual, but leave God out all together. I can choose to recognize I have a spirit and recognize there is more to things than I can see, but stop there and never try to find out exactly who God is. When I look at these types of spiritual practices I start to notice they have a similarity to the teachings of Jesus. Spiritualists speak of manifesting your dreams. I believe this is very possible for people to do. Jesus tells us if we have the faith to move a mountain it will move. Without God involved, it is the whims of my corrupt heart that I am manifesting. So even if I am capable of cultivating the faith needed to bring into existence my every desire, I know that without Him I have only brought myself even closer to destruction. The more power I would achieve this way, the more power I would crave. Soon I would realize that it was never my power at all but the powers that exist outside of my control. The powers of darkness seek to ensnare me in this way. They seek to lure me in by granting my sinful desires, creating an addiction to power that rivals that of any drug. Then just like a drug I must seek out more and more no matter the cost. Any power that comes without the love and guidance of God, is poison.

Jesus is the only way that I become free of my sinful nature. When I put my trust in Him, He shows me how to live. He gives me the same power that raised Him from the dead. The power He gives comes with a love that changes everything. His love is the difference.

Of all the things that move me in this life there is only one that lasts. There is One who moves with me through every season. There is One changes every moment. There is One who gives me life and then life again. There is One who allows me to live in His presence. There is One who my soul longs to worship for eternity.

90. HOPE KEEPS ME SWIMMING

Pure gold put in the fire comes out of it proved pure; genuine faith put through this suffering comes out proved genuine. When Jesus wraps this all up, it's your faith, not your gold that God will have on display as evidence of His victory. You never saw Him, yet you love Him. You still don't see Him, yet you trust Him- with laughter and singing. Because you kept on believing you'll get what you're looking forward to: total salvation.
I Peter 1:6-9 MSG

"There is nothing I would not do for you, Andrea." I hear these words often. I can not imagine words that would give me more hope than these. There is a completeness and a truth to the statement. I feel it in my very being. The God who created everything would do anything for me. If it were in my best interest, He would with a swipe of His hand wipe away all of existence leaving just He and I face to face. Sometimes when things are very difficult, I focus on Him and it feels like He has done this. I can see everything else melt away and there is nothing but He and I. There is a feeling this brings that I can not describe. As I write this I asked God for a word to help me describe this feeling. He gave it to me. The definition I heard was, when the unnecessary leaves, I hold purely what I need.

When I let go of the things that are clinging to me, screaming for my attention, demanding my thoughts and energy, I am left with Him. It is in this recognition that when all else is gone, it is Him still with me. I would sooner give up my air than Him. This is a realization I could have never had, a perfect feeling I could have never known with mere words. The truths of God are meant to be lived, not just talked about. Every joy, every trial, every moment lived with Him, brings wisdom and truth. Each moment changes me and shapes me into a better version of myself. A version that is pure and shiny and capable of reflecting Him.

91. A LIFE SUPREME

As obedient children, let yourself be pulled into a way of life shaped by God's life, a life energetic and blazing with holiness. God said, "I am holy; you be holy." You call out to God for help and He helps- He's a good Father that way. But don't forget, He's also a responsible Father, and won't let you get by with sloppy living. Your life is a journey you must travel with a deep consciousness of God.
I Peter 1:14-18 MSG

There is a toy at the park that is my favorite to play on with the girls. It looks like a really tall mushroom and it has handles all the way around the edge of the cap. The entire cap spins. It is fairly tall so kids need lifted up to reach. When we get on and start spinning pretty soon our legs are flying out to the side and we are holding on for dear life. It is thrilling and terrifying. If I lose my grip I fly out on to the ground for a very unpleasant landing. Even small children can recognize when their grip is failing and they need to be let down. God gave me this inner warning system to let me know what I am capable of and when I am in danger. Without seeking these limits I would never find them. When I find them, I can learn to push them in ways that cause me to grow.

When it is spiritual growth that is taking place things are different. I have internal alarms that have been conditioned by the world. Ones that tell me to trust in money, trust in my own abilities and work to save me, trust only in what I can verify with my senses. God shows me how to bypass these warnings. They are not from Him, they only bring me anxiety, fear, and trouble. This is not an easy process. The warnings feel very much the same as the one in my head at the park that says my grip is failing and I will soon fly off the toy and land in a pile of broken bones. Here though God reassures me and says my grip doesn't need to fail I just need to let go. When I let go, I fall. I knew I would fall, He told me what to expect. It doesn't change the fact that I can feel the very real sensation of falling. He holds my hands and looks me right in the eyes and reminds me who He is. My fear turns to excitement. I had to jump head first into what the world tells me to fear, in order to overcome it. I am once again holding onto only what I need, Him. Here I have peace.

92. MORE LIKE HIM

*Friends, when life gets really difficult, don't jump to
the conclusion that God isn't on the job. Instead, be glad that
you are in the very thick of what Christ experienced. This is a
spiritual refining process, with glory just around the corner.*
I Peter 4:12-13 MSG

After I let God tear down my life to the bare bones, I sort of stood there stoopified. I didn't not know how to make a move without asking Him first. The fact that He is always there to help me with every step of the day gave me confidence, and at the same time took away the crushing pressure of my responsibilities. So for a long while I went through my days stopping before every single next thing I would do, and asking Him what comes next. Lately He has been telling me that life is going to speed up, a lot. I need to choose confidence over caution. He reminded me that He is inside of me, a part of me. I do not have to stop to double check every single thought I have, making sure it is Him speaking to me and not myself. I know my voice is in there too and I am likely to act on it instead of His, so this is where I struggle with confidence. Again, He tells me "It's a good day for things to go wrong." Even if I do make a misstep there is nothing He can't turn for my good. In all actuality no misstep can ever be a misstep because He knows every step I will take before I take it.

With my girls, I want them to have everything I can give them that is good in life. For the most part when they ask for things, my answer is always yes. God is the same way. He wants to say yes to me, there is nothing He wouldn't do for me. This makes it all the more meaningful when the answer is no. Not only that, but occasionally hearing no, reminds me that He is capable and willing to tell me no and that I can and will hear him. So all of the times I hear "yes" make me more confident in His "no" and the times I hear "no" make me confident in all the times I hear "yes."

The other night as I was lying in bed He spoke to me with a picture of a kangaroo. The kangaroo had a baby in it's pouch. He told me it was time to hop along with Him instead of riding. This made me sad, and frustrated, and I cried. Life at this point is full of difficulties, there is nowhere I can look right now without seeing a problem that I do not know how to solve on my own. On top of this school is starting and activities that all take loads of time and money. He is the only thing keeping me from collapsing in on myself. Then He tells me to hop out of the pouch. I felt like He was telling me to start doing things on my own. He sat with me and let me process emotions.

Once my mind had quieted again, He told me something He says to me quite often "Don't you for even one second think that I am not going to take care of you in every single way." Then He reminded me that I am not supposed to be comfortable here, because I am not staying here. I am moving. This frustration and discomfort is what is preparing me to move. The more frustrating and the more uncomfortable the more I am growing. He also reminded me that He is never late. Sometimes He takes me down scenarios that I would consider worst case, just to remind me that even worst case is not bad with Him. I eventually realized that He was telling me He is actually going to be closer to me, I just need to trust Him enough to move confidently without second guessing every step.

The way He works often initially look like it will accomplish the opposite of what it is accomplishing. What I thought was Him pulling away from me and wanting me to be more independent, was actually Him pulling me closer and teaching me to rely on Him more completely.

93. WIDE EYED WONDER

"The lamp of the body is the eye. If therefore your eye is good, your whole body will be full of light. But if your eye is bad, your whole body will be full of darkness. If therefore the light that is in you is darkness, how great is that darkness!"
Matthew 6:22-23 NKJ

"Your eyes are windows into your body. If you open your eyes wide in wonder and belief, your body fills up with light. If you live squinty-eyed in greed and distrust, your body is a musty cellar. If you pull the blinds on your windows, what a dark life you will have!"
Matthew 6:22-23 MSG

The way I view the world has changed. I put an importance on things they did not used to have. In this way I am able to accomplish big things even in little things. When I see everything I do as being done for God, the mundane becomes the magnificent. I recognize my body as the temple of the Holy Spirit. Therefore, the way I treat my body becomes far more important than if it was just my meat suit that carried me around. The reasons for taking good care of it are more important than just how I look and feel. If my reason for taking care of my body was only to look good and feel good, then at some point age would begin to catch up to me and I might just thrown in the towel and pick up the brownies. Looking and feeling good are a nice by product of caring for my body but they are not the sole reason.

When I used to experience anything exceptional or

beautiful or special I would feel the need to whip out my phone and share photos. There was a need built into me to share the good things in my life, and to share them with more than just the people around me. Once I learned to recognize that God is with me in every step of every day that need was met. He not only shares in the physical moment, He shares my thoughts and feelings.

I have always been a people pleaser, and needed validation from the people around me. There was a need built into me to be loved. He loves me like no one else ever could. It is easy to get caught up in admiring the lives and people I see displayed on the television. The people that seem to have all the money, all the power, all the beauty captivate me. I searched for something bigger and better than the life I knew, bigger and better than myself. The lives they display are fleeting and hollow. God is power and might. When I have Him I need not look any further.

94. ABSOLUTELY EVERYTHING

*"But seek first the kingdom of God and His righteousness,
and all these things shall be added to you. Therefore, do not
worry about tomorrow, for tomorrow will worry about its
own things. Sufficient for the day is its own trouble."*
Matthew 6:33-34 NKJV

I know God is fully capable of accomplishing everything
He wants to accomplish without me. Still, He chooses to involve
me. I know from my experience as a mother, help from people
who have no idea how to help and need constant instruction, is
actually more work. This leads me to believe that He wants me
to be involved for my benefit, and that He must enjoy spending
time with me.

When I was very small and I would go to the amusement
park, rides like the merry go round and little cars that carry you
around a track were exciting. As I got older I needed more of a
thrill. It didn't take long before I was riding every ride I could,
the wilder the better.

As I grow in God, my walk with Him changes. He never
lets me get bored or stuck in a rut with Him. He invites me into
new challenges and joys. He is obviously capable of anything,
there is nothing He cannot do. His greatest joy seems to be found
in me. Of all the things He could do to find pleasure He chooses
to help me, to spend time loving me, this is His great joy. So
much so that He gave everything for me, and would do it again
if needed. He doesn't need me to help people and love people. He

wants to share what brings Him great joy with me. He wants me to experience every joy and all the goodness He has to offer.

This means as I trust him more, I let him prepare me and make me capable of carrying out more difficult but rewarding tasks. He can not send me to help others when I am not ready and might fall into temptation harming myself and the people I am meant to help. The preparation is hard. It challenges every part of me. It kills the parts that would destroy me. It grows new parts that make me stronger. All of it is uncomfortable. In the discomfort He holds me, He speaks to me, He reminds me there is nothing he would not do for me.

95. SWEPT AWAY

My little children, let us not love in word or in tongue, but in deed and in truth. And by this we know that we are of the truth, and shall assure our hearts before Him. For if our heart condemns us, God is greater than our heart, and knows all things. Beloved, if our heart does not condemn us, we have confidence toward God. And whatever we ask, we receive from Him, because we keep His commandments and do those things that are pleasing in His sight. And this is His commandment: that we should believe on the name of His Son Jesus Christ and love one another, as he gave us commandment.
I John 3:18-23 NKJV

My dear children let's not just talk about love; let's practice real love. This is the only way we'll know we're living truly, living in God's reality. It's also the way to shut down debilitating self-criticism, even when there is something to it. For God is greater than our worried hearts and knows more about us than we do, ourselves. And friends, once that's taken care of and we're no longer accusing or condemning ourselves, we're bold and free before God! We're able to stretch out our hands and receive what we asked for because we're doing what he said, doing what pleases him- Again this is God's command: to believe in His personally named Son, Jesus Christ. He told us to love each other in line with the original command. As we keep his commands, we live deeply and surely in him, and he lives in us. And this is how we experience his deep and abiding presence in us: by the spirit he gave us.
I John 3:18-24 MSG

Before I fully put my life on the altar as a living sacrifice, I was like a caterpillar crawling along. God watched me He loved me even then, He saw me as the butterfly I would become. I crawled along the earth stuck to the ground in a sort of monotonous dull way. Then I asked Him to take my crawling nose to the ground life, and give me something better. He wrapped me in a cocoon of Himself, and began to work.

Once He finished making me into a butterfly, He let me get used to my new body while still wrapped in the cocoon. Pretty soon He started to challenge me He would tell me "you're ready." Then show me how to begin to move and wiggle my new wings and body. Instead of the cocoon falling off and breaking away it just started to expand around me giving me room to flap my wings. Then it started to turn transparent, so that I have to work a little harder to see it still there, but now I can see the outside world too.

He couldn't keep me in that little cocoon forever, I would've gotten tired of it. He doesn't leave me though. He still surrounds me, I just have a little more space to flap my wings. I still see Him, but I see the outside world too. So I have to focus and not let the outside world distract me from the fact that He is still here with me. When I work to focus on Him, instead of the outside world, I feel His love, His presence, His guiding hand.

God contains pure emotion. He reminds me of this when I feel an overwhelming love for Him wash over me out of nowhere. He tells me "you love me because I loved you first." This is true in the literal sense. I can love Him because He loved me. It is true in another sense as well. When I surrender my life to Him, I become a part of Him and He is a part of me. When He looks at me with love I feel it. I don't just feel it, it overwhelms me, it penetrates down into my soul and then overflows back out reflecting into my life and into the world.

Now that I am a butterfly I am more sensitive to the way He moves. I can be lifted and carried by even the slightest breeze. Before when I was crawling along nose to the ground clinging for dear life, He followed and gently guided but for the most part I trudged along without much thought to Him. With wings, the entire sky has opened up and there is no telling where He will take me.

96. CREATOR

"For My thoughts are not your thoughts, nor are your ways My ways." says the Lord. "For as the heavens are higher than the earth, so are My ways higher than your ways, and My thoughts than your thoughts. For as the rain comes down, and the snow from heaven, and do not return there, but water the earth, and make it bring forth and bud, that it may give seed to the sower and bread to the eater, So shall my word be that goes forth from My mouth; It shall not return to me void, but it shall accomplish what I please, and it shall prosper in the thing for which I sent it. For you shall go out with joy, and be led out with peace; The mountains and the hills shall break forth into singing before you, and all the trees of the fields shall clap their hands. Instead of the thorn shall come up the cypress tree, and instead of the briar shall come up the myrtle tree; and it shall be to the Lord for a name, for an everlasting sign that shall not be cut off."
Isaiah 55:8-13

There are certain times of the year and after a rain when the road to my house gets little frogs hopping and flying through the air. They seem to be magentically drawn to the front of my car. Most of the time if they would just sit still until my car passed they would be fine. No, they hop at exactly the wrong moment and I hear a little thwack. Maybe if I inspected the car after I would see the remnants of frog, but I would rather not look. I continue about my day and forget all about the frog. I suppose at some point if the wind, rain or car wash didn't flick the little corpses off I would be driving around in a big mess.

The little frogs hopping in front of my car remind me of the negative and sinful thoughts that sometimes pop into my mind. There is no avoiding them they just fly out of nowhere smacking into my day. I could let myself feel bad about it, but why? It's already smacked the car, and there is really no way to avoid them. So I choose to continue down the road without a second thought. I know that these thoughts are not my fault, they are just part of living in this body. What would be my fault is if I held onto that thought like a creepy little stinky frog corpse and made it into something it is not. Jesus paid the price for my nature and my sin. I will make use of the precious gift He has given me and will not let sin take even an inch of space in my mind.

When my mind is free from sin, I can focus on the promises of God and what He speaks over my life. There will inevitably be negative thoughts that pop into my head to try and convince me that the things God has spoken over my life and to me are not true. I will let His mighty wind of truth blow them out of my mind. When I am left with the things He tells me, I am filled with hope, joy and an unstopably beautiful vision for the future.

97. MADE TO CONQUER

... My servant David, who kept My commandments and who followed Me with all his heart, to do only what was right in My eyes

I Kings 14:8 NKJV

There are certain stories and character traits that are unquestionably good and admirable. I love movies about heroes and their journeys. I can watch in admiration as I watch the underdog fight to the top, or as heroes are knocked down to a rock bottom only to fight their way back to the top. It speaks to something in me, something that knows there is more, there is greatness to be achieved and adventure to be had. I longed to fight my way to a better life, to greatness. The only problem was that the world told me it was a fight that didn't exist. There was no real fight to be had. Instead, I was taught to memorize the way the world wanted me to see, and follow its rules. If I complied then I might move up in society and be rewarded. The world taught me that the real fight, was fighting my inner desire for more and for adventure. That in order to succeed and be a respected member of society I would need to tamp that down and learn to live by the world's rules.

The only problem is that desire can not be killed. So the world feeds alcohol, drugs, television, social media, sex, things to help me quiet the voice inside me that screams for more. Then once I am a slave to my sin it holds up a mirror and tells me how weak and pathetic I am. I can try to control things on my own. I can work very hard and make money. I can diet and exercise and shape my body into what the world thinks is acceptable. The more I achieve here, the more I want. It is only a matter of time before something happens and my body does not cooperate, or the dollar fails and my money is gone. Even if I manage to keep up my appearance and my bank account, the more I have the greater the fear of losing it. So I become a slave to my achievments in much the same way I would've been a slave to food or drugs or sex. Either way I end up in chains. The good news is God loves an underdog as much as I do. The only way out of this is to take the heroes journey. I must let go of everything I hold onto and free fall into the arms of God. It is exactly the kind of wildly exciting, excruciatingly rewarding life that I not only need, but desperately want. It is in the crushing death of my flesh that I am given new strength to rise again victorious. Better than any story, better than any movie, it is what I was made for.

Made in the USA
Columbia, SC
01 October 2024

42741884R00124